MW01098806

Time Shift

Managing Time to Create a Life You Love

Eugene Dupuis

Copyright © 2001 by Eugene Dupuis. All rights reserved.

No part of this publication may be reproduced or transmitted in any form or by any means, electronic or mechanical, including photocopying, recording or any other storage and retrieval system, without the written permission of the author.

The Achievement Institute
1078 Bennett Road
Bowmanville, Ontario
Canada L1C 3K5
416-254-6196
www.achievement-institute.ca

Art Direction   Paul Andrew Smith
Graphic Design   IMAGE communication & design
Cover Photography   Paul Andrew Smith
Photo page 171   David Lee

National Library of Canada Cataloguing in Publication Data

Dupuis, Eugene, 1957-
    Time shift : managing time to create a life you love

Includes bibliographical references and index.

ISBN 1-55212-960-8
    1. Time management. I. Title.

BF637.T5D86 2001   640'.43   C2001-903451-2

TRAFFORD

Suite 6E, 2333 Government St., Victoria, B.C. V8T 4P4, CANADA
Phone   250-383-6864   Toll-free   1-888-232-4444 (Canada & US)
Fax   250-383-6804   E-mail   sales@trafford.com
Web site   www.trafford.com   TRAFFORD PUBLISHING IS A DIVISION OF TRAFFORD HOLDINGS LTD.
Trafford Catalogue #01-0362   www.trafford.com/robots/01-0362.html

10   9   8   7   6   5   4   3   2

Acknowledgements

Nothing in this world is accomplished without the support, lessons and assistance of those around us. Although the words in this book are mine, they are simply a reflection of hundreds of thousands of words and lessons that I have been fortunate enough to digest over 25 years of studies. I'd like to acknowledge my debt to all those in the personal development field that have come before me and graciously paved the way for a smooth journey.

I would like to thank my family - Sharon, my life partner, for supporting my dreams in the face of adversity; and my children Alyson and Christopher, whose generosity of love and spirit has me see sunshine on cloudy days.

I am indebted to Paul Andrew Smith for the endless hours and creativity that he poured into designing this book, and whose efforts reflect a commitment to quality every step of the way; to Jim Clemmer, Michael LeBoeuf, Brian Tracy, Robin Sharma, Tim Breithaupt, Jim Rohrbach, and Bill Blake for kind words and support that I will never forget; to Mark Shapiro, Marina Glogovac and Bruce Gale, whose early confidence in the teachings of this program were priceless; to my close friends Guy Lepage and Steve Fitzgerald, who put things into perspective by providing honest and sincere feedback; to Tim Whittaker and Betty Carr for empowering me to learn and achieve meaningful accomplishments and life lessons; and to the many participants I have been fortunate enough to coach through 'The Masters Program', each of whom have taught me and enriched my life.

Eugene Dupuis

Introduction

The most simple ideas, if we use them to generate action, can change our lives. This book is full of simple ideas that can change your life.

People around the world are searching for ways to get more done in less time, to generate more fulfillment from their work and to make something of their lives. They are experimenting with new paradigms, new technology, new jobs and new partners. They are looking for the answer to that age-old question; "What am I here for?"

The answer does not always lie in changing our environment ... but in changing ourselves, the way we act, and the way we look at the world. The insights and exercises in this book will challenge the way you look at the world, it will challenge the way you think, and it will challenge the way you spend your time.

I first met Eugene Dupuis when he called on Nightingale-Conant to provide insight, resources and coaching to get him to the next level in his training career. Since then I've seen him develop these timeless principles in Metropolitan Toronto with members of the publishing profession, and establish The Achievement Institute in nearby Durham Region. From there he began to powerfully train public and private sector executives across the country and from a variety of backgrounds.

The results were significant. Executives started fine-tuning their time, working on actions and activities that generated significant results in relatively short periods of time. They began to understand the connection between goal setting, daily planning and personal fulfillment. His clients' productivity increased, their stress decreased, and they began to experience more joy and fulfillment in their work. Workshops, speeches and follow-up programs added more to his research base, and his work is now recognized as one of the most powerful time management programs in the country.

Time Management training has been around for ages. There are hundreds of books, manuals and tapes available, and they all carry some value. This book, however, is about you and how you can modify your actions and behaviours to do more than just manage your time. Managing time is for beginners. Managing yourself to create a life you love is for winners. This book is for winners!

Jim Rohrbach
(www.SuccessSkills.com)
Success Skills Coach, Nightingale-Conant Corporation
and Author of 'Business Success Skills'

I am very impressed! You have created the quintessential manual for those who wish to be high performing achievers, and who are prepared to learn, and practice the skills you have developed.

The more I advanced through your book, the more enthusiastic I became. It is much more than a time management text, it is more a manual for a successful high performing life. As an instructor in time management for over 20 years, I fully agree with your premise that time management is essentially self management. Many practitioners will agree with the statement, but far fewer go on to demonstrate the principles of self management as you have done. You indicate that one's ability to generate results are based on attitudes, actions and behaviours. But more than that, you then demonstrate, through activities and exercises, how that can be accomplished. One statement you have used that I will quote again and again is: 'We are 100% responsible for our lives, and acceptance of this responsibility, without excuses, is a true hallmark of peak performing, high achieving, self actualized human beings.'

There are many aspects of the book that are simply outstanding - among them, the importance of goals; balancing goals; your goal setting checklist; personal habits; procrastination; reducing reading time; abuse of time especially email; and the wisdom contained in the section on Fru-Fru or Everything Else.

In summary, you have done much more than outline the techniques for managing time, you have created a superb manual for people who wish to be 'peak performing, high achieving, self actualized human beings', and who will lead balanced happy lives.

Bill Blake,
Norquest Learning Systems

Contents

Will This Workbook Work for You?

You are holding the combined material and exercises from the powerful time management coaching program, Time and Self Management; The Masters Program™.

Since this program was introduced in early 2000, it has improved the lives of all who have applied the lessons as coached by The Achievement Institute. Read what they have to say about their results at www.Achievement-Institute.ca

It will work for you too ... you can get the same results ... if you do the work. But you will have to be extremely disciplined because you will be coaching yourself.

This workbook has been developed to generate results for those who take action. If you are prepared to take action, then complete the following steps and enjoy the results. This will work for you whether you're a file clerk, salesperson, entrepreneur, manager or president.

Good luck, take action, and work with confidence.

*"He wants to buy an exercise bicycle
with a motor on it"*

Step One

Complete the Preliminary Reading. Don't skip this step thinking that you'll save time and get right to what's really important. If you do nothing but read the first 10 pages and implement three of the suggestions, you will still significantly improve your use of time.

Step Two

Complete all the Preliminary Exercises, in order. These will identify your highest priority needs, and have you set objectives for further reading and action. If you want this workbook to make a real difference, do all the work before reading any of the other chapters.

Step Three

Read each chapter in order, complete any additional exercises that you might find enlightening, and implement suggestions that seem appropriate for you.

Step Four

Do something .. anything .. to improve your use of time. Don't just read the words - do the work. This is a workbook and it is guaranteed to empower you to create a life you love, but only if you do the work! The more work you do, the more fulfillment you create.

Step Five

Complete your Behavioural Contract and reward yourself when you earn it.

Step Six

Share the book, and what you've learned, with friends, family and peers so that as many people as possible create a life that they love. If it has helped you in any way, send me a note.

If we can improve the process for the next edition, send me a note as well. to mail@achievement-institute.ca

"From your parents you learn love and laughter and how to put one foot in front of the other. But when books are opened you discover that you have wings."
Helen Hayes

Time Shift

Managing Time to Create a Life You Love

"If you can spare the time Williams,
I'd like to see you in my office"

chapter one

Preliminary Reading

"Time is the inexplicable raw material of everything. With it, all is possible; without it, nothing. The supply of time is truly a daily miracle, an affair genuinely astonishing when examined.

You wake up in the morning, and lo! your purse is magically filled with twenty-four hours of the un-manufactured tissue of the universe of your life! It is yours. It is the most precious of possessions ... No one can take it from you. It can't be stolen, and no one receives more or less.

In the realm of time there is no aristocracy of wealth or intellect. Genius is never rewarded with even an extra hour a day. And there is no punishment. Waste your infinitely precious commodity as much as you will, and the supply will never be withheld from you. Moreover, you cannot draw on the future - it's impossible to get into debt! You can only waste the passing moment. You cannot waste tomorrow; it is kept for you. You cannot waste the next hour; it is kept for you.

I have said the affair was a miracle. Is it not?

You have to live on this twenty-four hours of daily time. Within it, you have to spin health, pleasure, money, content, respect, and the evolution of your immortal soul. Its right use, its most effective use, is a matter of the highest urgency, and the most thrilling actuality. Everything depends on that: Your happiness, the elusive prize that we all reach for, depends on that.

"If one cannot arrange that an income of twenty-four hours a day shall exactly cover all proper items of expenditure, one's whole life is muddled indefinitely. We shall never have any more time. We have, and have always had, all the time there is."

Arnold Bennett

Overview

You do have enough time!
You have all the time there is. You have the same 1440 minutes today that everyone else has. What you don't have are the skills of managing yourself through that time. This program covers the tricks, tips and techniques you need to take charge of your time.

When you truly commit to learning, you can master anything you put your mind to. You must accept complete responsibility for learning what it takes to manage your time. This program shows you how to learn.

"Action is the proper fruit of knowledge"
Proverb

Many people have an idea of what they would like out of their lives, but don't effectively work towards accomplishing it. They wander around their world aimlessly, wondering why they don't get what they want. You're just a dreamer unless you use your time to accomplish meaningful goals. This program covers effective goal setting and accomplishment.

It's all about habits
Most good time management techniques run counter to personal habit patterns. To make progress, you have to look squarely at your own work habits and systems and be willing to improve them. Unlearning old habits and learning new ones is difficult - but essential. This program introduces powerful new work skills and techniques and shows you how to turn them into habits.

Accept personal responsibility
It is particularly difficult for some people to accept the reality that they themselves are to blame for many of their time problems. Instead, we find it much eas-

ier to blame drop-in visitors, paperwork, telephone interruptions and crises of one form or another. This program enables you to take responsibility and shows you how to manage the people and things in your life that waste time.

Time Management is Self Management

Time Management is not about time in the abstract; it's about what we can accomplish with time. We cannot manage our time, we can only manage ourselves in relation to time. We cannot control how much time we have, we can only control what we do with it. Time management is self management. It's not easy ... however it is worth the effort, for the benefits are profound. We have more time for family, reduced stress, improved personal productivity, and the realization of our goals.

How to Get the Most Out of this Workbook

1. If you want to get the most out of this book, there is one non-negotiable, indispensable requirement, the absence of which will undermine any efforts to better manage your time. It is the deep driving desire to obtain more fulfillment in your life, and the complete realization and belief that the way to get more fulfillment is to master yourself first. You must accept sole responsibility for who you are and the choices that you make around the use of your time.

"He who dares to teach must never cease to learn."
John Cotton Dana

2. Don't just read the material, apply what you learn as soon as you learn it.

3. Implement an integrated time management system as instructed, and be disciplined in making it a daily habit.

4. Focus singlemindidly on completing this book before picking up any other self-help books.

5. Make the decision right now that you will become excellent at time management skills. This will program your mind for adapting new ideas.

6. See and feel yourself as a Master of time. Visualize yourself as being more effective than you have ever been in your life.

7. Act 'as if' you are already using your time to its maximum effectiveness. Soon you will be.

8. Notice how others effectively use time and emulate them.

9. Imagine you will be teaching time management to others six months from now, and share what you learn as you learn it.

10. Decide what you have to do, establish their order of importance, and do first things first to completion.

11. Manage yourself minute by minute because the present is all you can control. Take care of the minutes and the hours and days will take care of themselves.

12. Be patient ... start in one area at a time, practice the techniques of establishing new habits, and take the full 21 days it takes to establish each one.

13. Be kind on yourself and don't try to change too much at once ... if you find yourself overwhelmed, take a breather and make an appointment with yourself for the day that you will resume your efforts.

Tall Tales on Time Management
(12 points of misinformation)

1. Time Management is just common sense. If I'm doing well at my job, I must be managing my time just fine.

2. I work better under pressure. Time management would take away that edge.

3. If I use an appointment calendar and to-do list, that's enough.

4. Time management is complicated.

5. Time management takes away my freedom - it eliminates spontaneity.

6. Time management might be good for some type of work, but I'm creative and can't be tied to a routine.

7. Time management takes too much time. I don't have time to do what it takes.

8. I have different ambitions than most. My time management needs aren't the same as others'.

9. I write everything down, so I'm already organized.

10. The only way to get more done is to work harder.

11. Time management won't help naturally disorganized people.

12. In order to be fully productive, I have to achieve complete control over how my time is spent.

"Excuse me. I wonder if you would
give me a little push?"

chapter two

Preliminary Exercises

The Reader/Author Agreement

Congratulations on making the commitment to improve your Time and Self-Management. You are on the road to taking control of your time and your life, and this agreement is where the proverbial 'rubber meets the road'. This is the place and time for you to clarify the intensity of your commitment. What kind of results do you want out of this workbook, and how much work are you willing to put into it? Make this agreement with the author and post it somewhere that you can see every day until you've achieved what you've set out to achieve. Completion of this agreement holds significant power through the fact that it makes your commitment more real by getting it out into the world.

Basic Results

I want to improve my use of time, and will do any work that fits into my schedule and routines that immediately appear to make a difference. I will accept whatever suggestions seem to make sense, but prefer to interpret things over time and implement new ideas at a slow and comfortable pace. I will take action that makes better use of my time if it fits my personality and existing priorities. I commit to selectively read this book and do whatever exercises I have time for.

Participant Signature _____ Date _____

Moderate Results

I am committed to making better use of my time, and will do the work necessary to make a difference. I will read the book with an open mind, looking for insights into how I might be more productive. I will take action to make better use of my time every day until I complete reading the book. I will introduce an integrated time management system as outlined, complete all of the assessment profiles, complete all of the suggested exercises based on the results of this assessment, and implement at least six suggestions introduced in this book.

Participant Signature _____ Date _____

Powerful Results

I am truly committed to having a breakthrough in my use of time, and will do all of the work necessary to create transformation. I will study the text and exercises with an eager, open mind at all times, reading as if the quality of my life depended on it. I will take significant actions to make better use of my time every day for the next three months. I will follow all of the instructions in the introduction on how to get the most out of this book. I will introduce an integrated time management system, complete all of the assessment profiles, complete all of the suggested exercises based on the results of this assessment, read the complete book twice, listen to a personal development audio tape set on success/achievement, and introduce at least 12 suggestions introduced in this book within the next 12 weeks.

Participant Signature _____ Date _____

Author's Signature

How Well Do You Master Your Time?

This questionnaire will allow you to evaluate your current work habits as they relate to each of the time and self-management categories covered in this book. The results will allow you to focus on the exercises and suggestions for most effectively improving your use of time.

Instructions:

Read each statement carefully, as some of them are worded positively and some are worded negatively. Consider how much you agree or disagree with each statement as it relates to you, and circle the score under one of four responses: Strongly Disagree, Mildly Disagree, Mildly Agree, Strongly Agree. Add your total score for each category.

You'll want to be aware of the categories you scored the lowest in, and all of the statements for which you only scored 1 point. These are areas which require your particular attention.

	Strongly Agree	Mildly Agree	Mildly Disagree	Strongly Disagree
Attitudes and Beliefs				
1. I believe that the life I live is a life that I create.	4	3	2	1
2. I believe that my outlook and attitude determine most of the results in my life.	4	3	2	1
3. There are people and circumstances that have held me back in life.	1	2	3	4
4. I have confidence that I can do anything I set my mind to.	4	3	2	1
5. I've achieved most of what I've wanted to up to now.	4	3	2	1
6. I often feel that there isn't enough time to get everything of importance done.	1	2	3	4
7. I am mostly satisfied with my life.	4	3	2	1
8. I don't learn or adopt new things very easily.	1	2	3	4
9. I am very disciplined and have strong willpower. . . .	4	3	2	1
10. I know myself fairly well.	4	3	2	1

TOTAL _____

	Strongly Agree	Mildly Agree	Mildly Disagree	Strongly Disagree
Stress Control				
1. There are some things beyond my control that really cause me stress.	1	2	3	4
2. I have a need to control and have trouble completely 'letting go'.	1	2	3	4
3. I'm always in a rush and have too much to do.	1	2	3	4
4. I live a healthy lifestyle with a good diet and regular exercise.	4	3	2	1

25

	Strongly Agree	Mildly Agree	Mildly Disagree	Strongly Disagree
5. I take quiet time for myself, away from distractions every day.	4	3	2	1
6. I have some habits that I really don't like.	1	2	3	4
7. I worry quite a bit.	1	2	3	4
8. I often have trouble concentrating on one thing a time.	1	2	3	4
9. I have very rewarding relationships with people.	4	3	2	1
10. I often enjoy what I'm doing so much that I lose track of time.	4	3	2	1

TOTAL _____

Personal Goals and Purpose

	Strongly Agree	Mildly Agree	Mildly Disagree	Strongly Disagree
1. I know the legacy I want to leave, or how I want to be remembered.	4	3	2	1
2. I believe that mission statements serve no real purpose.	1	2	3	4
3. I have a written set of short and long term goals.	4	3	2	1
4. I can achieve my goals without having a disciplined system.	1	2	3	4
5. I know what I want out of life and do something every day towards getting them.	4	3	2	1
6. My life is balanced.	4	3	2	1
7. I'm relatively unfulfilled right now.	1	2	3	4
8. I resent spending most of my time on other people's priorities.	1	2	3	4
9. I reward myself for attaining difficult tasks.	4	3	2	1
10. I'm proud of the things for which I've worked long and hard	4	3	2	1

TOTAL _____

Planning and Implementation

	Strongly Agree	Mildly Agree	Mildly Disagree	Strongly Disagree
1. I write important things down on 'post-it notes', or pieces of paper.	1	2	3	4
2. I often get distracted from my plan for the day, jumping from one demand to another.	1	2	3	4
3. I get everything of urgency and importance done between 8 am and 6 pm.	4	3	2	1
4. I often feel overwhelmed.	1	2	3	4
5. I work on my most important activity, and fully concentrate on it to its completion.	4	3	2	1
6. I write out a prioritized list of actions and activities for each day.	4	3	2	1
7. I have a problem with uncertain or constantly changing priorities.	1	2	3	4
8. I regularly schedule private time to work on things.	4	3	2	1

	Strongly Agree	Mildly Agree	Mildly Disagree	Strongly Disagree
9. I prefer to do things myself because I can do them better and faster.	1	2	3	4
10. I always know what to do next, even in the smallest window of time.	4	3	2	1

TOTAL _____

Personal Habits

	Strongly Agree	Mildly Agree	Mildly Disagree	Strongly Disagree
1. People have recognized how much I've developed over the years.	4	3	2	1
2. I often postpone actions and activities that I don't like.	1	2	3	4
3. I have trouble starting big jobs.	1	2	3	4
4. I often say No to the requests of others, and do it with courtesy.	4	3	2	1
5. My workspace is a mess.	1	2	3	4
6. I'm considered a perfectionist.	1	2	3	4
7. I listen powerfully, giving complete undivided attention to the speaker.	4	3	2	1
8. I can't keep up with all my reading.	1	2	3	4
9. My written communication is timely and succinct.	4	3	2	1
10. I'm truly committed to introducing new habits that will make better use of my time.	4	3	2	1

TOTAL _____

Priorities

	Strongly Agree	Mildly Agree	Mildly Disagree	Strongly Disagree
1. Incoming email dictates much of what I do at the beginning of each day.	1	2	3	4
2. Distractions and interruptions often keep me from my work.	1	2	3	4
3. I have difficulty limiting office chit-chat.	1	2	3	4
4. I close my office door (or would if I had one) several times a day.	4	3	2	1
5. I answer just about every incoming phone call.	1	2	3	4
6. I attend just about every meeting I'm invited to.	1	2	3	4
7. I regularly limit my participation in meetings to agenda items that concern me.	4	3	2	1
8. I'm always looking for ways to save time for myself and others.	4	3	2	1
9. I think I waste my time on some things.	1	2	3	4
10. I usually don't notice people walking by or waiting to speak with me.	4	3	2	1

TOTAL _____

Write the three categories with the lowest scores on your personal profile summary at the end of these preliminary exercises.

Mastery Self-Analysis

This short exercise has you identify the gaps that exist between where you think you are now, and where you want to be. You will notice that the categories match those in the previous exercise, but this profile will indicate what you are truly motivated to improving, and therefore more likely to commit time and effort towards.

"If you have knowledge, let others light their candles by it."
Margaret Fuller

Indicate your present and desired level of mastery in each area from 1-10 (10 being a Master).

	Present Mastery	Desired Mastery
I. Attitudes and Beliefs		
Faith and Confidence	_____	_____
The Science of Personal Achievement	_____	_____
Acceptance of 100% Responsibility	_____	_____
Ability to Learn	_____	_____
Positive Mental Attitude	_____	_____
Self-Discipline	_____	_____
2. Stress Control		
Ability to Control Your Stress	_____	_____
Sense of Overwhelm	_____	_____
Worry	_____	_____
Living Life in the Fast Lane	_____	_____
Diet and Exercise	_____	_____
Relaxation Techniques	_____	_____
'Flow' and Being 'Present to The Moment'	_____	_____
Relationship Building	_____	_____
3. Personal Goals and Purpose		
Leaving a Legacy	_____	_____
Living a Life with Purpose	_____	_____
Goal Setting Skills and Techniques	_____	_____
Goal Planning and Achievement	_____	_____
4. Planning and Implementation		
Effective Time Management System	_____	_____
Action Lists.	_____	_____
Prioritizing	_____	_____
Doing First Things First	_____	_____
Scheduling Private, Uninterrupted Time	_____	_____

Sense of Urgency .... _____   _____
Daily Planning .... _____   _____
Effective Delegation .... _____   _____

5. Personal Habits

Creating New Habits.......................... _____   _____
Procrastination .... _____   _____
Perfectionism .... _____   _____
Powerful Listening .... _____   _____
Saying No................................... _____   _____
Effective Work Space .... _____   _____
Reading Time .... _____   _____
Writing...................................... _____   _____

6. Priorities

Email Overwhelm .... _____   _____
Controlling Interruptions .... _____   _____
Controlling the Telephone .... _____   _____
Reduce Meeting Time .... _____   _____

Highlight the 6 items above that have the biggest gaps between existing and desired Mastery. Write them on your personal profile summary at the end of these preliminary exercises.

Advance Avoidance Strategies

How can you avoid being successful this week? What are you responsible for that could stop you in your desire to be more productive with your time? Write out ten things you control that could stop you from implementing the techniques suggested in this book. Make sure you list only the things that you can control.

Avoidance Strategy	Probability Order
_____	# _____
_____	# _____
_____	# _____
_____	# _____
_____	# _____
_____	# _____
_____	# _____
_____	# _____
_____	# _____
_____	# _____

Now, number these in order of their probability of appearing, then write the top three on your personal profile summary at the end of the preliminary exercises.

Here are some sample answers given by seminar participants.
- I won't be open to new ideas, thinking the way I've always done it is the best
- I will be afraid of offending people if I don't give them all the time they need
- My office setup is not conducive
- I can't concentrate on one thing at a time
- I'll know what I should do, I just won't do it
- I'll play the victim and refuse to acknowledge that I am completely responsible
- I'll waste time chatting with people
- I'll be overwhelmed and not know which ideas to implement
- I'll have too many fires to put out
- My boss won't 'buy in' to my new time management ideas
- I have too much to do that I can't control
- I'll be judgmental and critical of new ideas

Identify Your Bad Habits

Habits are amazing. Few of us could explain rationally why we do certain things the way we do. We've been doing them that way for so long that we do them without thinking. When it comes to the pattern of how we use our time, habits can be subtle yet particularly damaging.

Sally reads her mail first thing every morning; she's always done it that way and she says it eases her into the day.

William keeps two calendars, one for business appointments and one for his personal schedule; he started it on his very first job when he received two appointment books as graduation gifts.

James writes everything down. He thinks he learned the habit from the very first personal development book that he ever read. No matter where he is or what he is doing, he'll grab a scrap of paper or sticky note to jot down anything he has to remember.

Margaret has a well established routine for correspondence. She writes her letters and interoffice memos in longhand on ruled pads (she claims she thinks better that way), has her assistant type up a draft, revises the draft, reviews the final copy for mistakes, and finally signs it.

Can you spot the mistakes?

There is probably nothing in Sally's mail that can't wait until the afternoon. If she put her first hour on her top priority task, she would be far more productive.

Margaret could cut her correspondence time by at least 66% if she would type, correct and edit on her own computer, all at one sitting.

James wastes valuable time trying to track down all his little pieces of paper, and often forgets to follow through on important details. It started years ago when he forgot that his development book actually directed him to write everything down in an integrated planning system, not on separate pieces of paper.

As for William, he acknowledges he frequently gets tangled up in overlapping commitments, but he ascribes this to carelessness, instead of a cumbersome system.

Look at Your Own Habits

Take a close look at the way you conduct yourself throughout the day. What do you do the same way every day? What habits have you fallen into that hinder rather than create maximum productivity? Don't force yourself to change at this point ... just take a close, honest look at yourself and write down five of your bad habits. Select the three that you are most committed to changing and write them on your personal profile summary at the end of the preliminary exercises.

Bad habits

_____

_____

_____

Performance Needs Analysis

It is our strongest motivations, our deepest desires related to work, that provide the key to peak performance. The ability to identify and adopt behaviours that simultaneously match our strongest motivations and bring value to our employer, propels us from mediocrity to joy and productivity at work. The following questions will help you identify these common areas. Identify the things that bring you joy and bring value to your employer, then do what it takes to spend most of your time on these activities.

1. What would you do if you didn't have to work?

_____

_____

2. What do you want to be remembered for in your work?

_____

_____

3. What is it you do that provides the most value to your employer?

_____

_____

4. What do you do of value that makes you happy in your work?

_____

_____

5. If you could spend more time on anything of value what would it be?

_____

_____

Finding more fulfillment in your work is as simple as spending more time on these activities you have just identified. When you plan your day, plan to do more of this!

Personal Profile Summary

This summary highlights your personal development options as uncovered in the previous pages. These are the areas that require particular attention in order for you to improve the effective use of your time. Refer to this summary regularly as you read the following pages ... look for and implement any techniques suggested for developing these areas and this book will have a profound impact on your life.

Development Alternatives

Three categories with the lowest scores from 'How Well do You Master Your Time?

1._____
2._____
3._____

Six items with the biggest gaps from 'Mastery Self Analysis'

1._____
2._____
3._____
4._____
5._____
6._____

Top three entries from 'Advance Avoidance Strategies'

1._____
2._____
3._____

Three worst habits you're committed to changing from 'Bad Habits'

1._____
2._____
3._____

Personal Achievement Objectives

I'm sure that you'd like to fix everything that appears to be wrong, and do it as soon as possible. But there's something that's absolutely critical for you to understand right now. You are 100% OK just the way you are. You were born completely whole, you still are whole, and your self-worth should not be judged by how well, or how poorly you do at anything. Feel great about yourself, because there is nothing to fix about you.

You do, however, generate results in your life based on your attitudes, actions and behaviours. These three Personal Achievement Objectives have you focus on the attitudes, actions and behaviours that will most significantly improve the results you generate in your life.

Review the fifteen development opportunities in your Personal Profile Summary on the previous page. What areas are repeated throughout the list? What areas are you seriously motivated to improve? Choose three areas that are most meaningful to you and write them in the space below. **Do it now.**

1. _____
2. _____
3. _____

Now write these three on a sheet of paper and post them where you can see them every day. Do it now, and don't read anymore until you do. If you have a dayplanner that you use, write them in there every morning to reinforce your commitment to developing this part of your life.

Tell yourself every night and every morning for the next three weeks that you are developing these areas, and that the work you do on them will empower you to create a life that you love. **Commit right now to affirming this twice a day for the next three weeks.**

Now proceed to read this book, do the exercises, and **implement any suggestions that even remotely impact these three areas.**

The Willpower Exercise

Doing things you don't normally do stretches your willpower, giving you the strength and confidence to achieve tremendous personal growth and accomplishment. These exercises will challenge you to move outside your comfort zone and do things you are not accustomed to. Some of them require an effort of will to actually do, others are quite simple, but the willpower comes in trying to do them every day.

Follow through on as many as possible of these simple exercises for the next week. Put the workbook away, move outside of your comfort zone for seven days, then come back and start reading about self management.

- When you are tempted to say something that you would normally share, hold back, don't say it.

- When you want to postpone doing something that you normally delay, do it right now.

- Do something simple that you normally wouldn't do - for example take your coffee or tea differently, contribute in some way at home that you don't normally do without being asked.

- At a restaurant, order something you've never even considered eating before, or ask if you can order something that is not on the menu.

- Talk to at least one stranger every day for the rest of the week.

- Set your alarm 10 minutes earlier than normal, and get out of bed immediately after waking up. Do this for the rest of the week.

- Say No to something that you really want to do, like watching your favourite tv show, or reading something for the pleasure of it.

- Take a different route to work and home again.

- Turn your car radio off for the rest of the week. Instead, listen to a personal development tape.

- Drink 6 bottles of water (500 ml size) tomorrow.

"You know, we're just not reaching
that guy."

chapter three

Self Management...

Attitudes and Beliefs

How the World Works

"The world has a way of giving what is demanded of it. If you are frightened and look for failure and poverty, you will get them, no matter how hard you may try to succeed. Lack of faith in yourself, in what life will do for you, cuts you off from the good things of the world. Expect victory and you make victory. Nowhere is this truer than in business life, where bravery and faith bring both material and spiritual rewards."

Dr. Preston Bradley

People flounder along from moment to moment, crisis to crisis, succeeding sometimes in spite of themselves. Less than 10% are happy with their jobs, less than 4% are financially independent. Our education system sorely lacks training in life skills that lead to success.

Why are some people more adept than others at managing themselves to a life of joy? Some succeed due to intellect, some as a result of higher education, but most are no different than you or me. Many have just done more with what they have. The majority of successful people have simply applied themselves with more determination, have worked both smarter and harder, have accepted their responsibilities and challenges, and have developed the attitudes that generate success.

These peak performers have generated outstanding results within the context of human nature.... within our world and the way it works. Most would agree that in order to influence the direction of our lives, we have to understand how we operate, how the mind works, what principles, laws and concepts rule us as human beings. This awareness tells us what commitments, effort and attitudes are required in order to achieve the things we want from life.

Brian Tracy, in Psychology of Achievement, effectively summarizes these basic underlying principles of the universe as the following laws which determine how our lives transpire.

The law of control

Those with a strong sense that they control what happens to them in life feel less stress and move much more decisively towards their goals.

The law of cause and effect

Our lives, relationships, happiness and performance are all the result of who we are and what we do. We create our future through our actions and behaviours. We cause the effects.

The law of belief

Whatever we believe, with conviction, becomes our reality. We have the power to create from belief.

"You cannot run away from a weakness; you must sometime fight it out or perish; and if that be so, why not now, and where you stand?"
Robert Louis Stevenson

The law of expectation

Whatever we expect with confidence becomes our self-fulfilling prophecy. High expectations create high levels of accomplishment. Winners make a habit of manufacturing their own positive expectations. They expect things to work out well, and as a result they do.

The law of attraction

Each human being is a living magnet ... we invariably attract into our lives the people and circumstances that match our dominant thoughts. We see that which we look for. By controlling the content of our conscious minds we can control who or what is attracted to us. We become what we think.

All that we achieve in our lives is the result of our attitudes ... how we view ourselves and the world around us. It is our attitudes that generate our joy and our sorrow, that create accomplishment or defeat ... that reflect who we are and what we stand for.

Individuals who become critically aware of their attitudes, and do what it takes to improve them, are unstoppable.

Unfortunately, there's no such thing as a quick-fix formula. It takes a consistent effort to create positive transformation. That's why more than 90% of people who attend short-term seminars see no lasting improvement in their lives. They don't make a consistent effort!

Controlling your attitudes and beliefs about the way the world works gives you the power to create a life that you love.

What it Takes to Create Success

It takes effort to create success, with this workbook and in our lives. There are common behaviours and characteristics that lend themselves to creating achievement, and if you've got them, you're several steps ahead of the crowd. Here's what some of the experts found about high achievers.

The Harvard Business School conducted a study to determine the common characteristics of peak performers. The evidence they found is clear ... that most people can be successful if they are willing to learn what is necessary, commit to doing what it takes, and focus on performance. Here are the attributes the study found in highly successful people:

100% acceptance of responsibility
They didn't blame others, the economy, the competition, or their company for their performance. They accepted full responsibility, and took any necessary action.

Above average ambition
These people had a deep desire to succeed, which affected priorities, how they spent their time, with whom they associated, etc.

"O Lord, Thou givest us everything, at the price of effort."
Leonardo Da Vinci

High levels of empathy
Peak performers have the ability to put themselves in others' shoes, imagine needs and concerns, and respond correctly.

Intensely goal oriented
Always knowing what they were going after, and how much progress they were making kept distractions from sidetracking highly successful people.

Above-average will power and determination
No matter how tempted they were to give up, they persisted towards goals ... self-discipline was a key.

Impeccable integrity
They spoke and acted consistent with their beliefs. No matter what the temptation, these people resisted, and gained the ongoing trust of others.

Ron Willingham, President of Integrity Systems of Phoenix Arizona, after training and observing tens of thousands of successful people in 48 different countries, found these four main traits they have in common.

Goal Clarity
Specific, measurable goals or objectives of what they want to be, do, earn, accomplish, gain or possess.

Achievement Drive
The desire or drive to achieve goals. Its energy. It's released from within when they have clear, believable goals that excite them.

Emotional Intelligence
Capacity for recognizing their own feelings and those of others, for motivating themselves, and for successfully managing their own emotions and relationships.

Social Skills
The ability to move in and out of social situations with grace and ease ... to ask the right questions and listen to people ... to gain empathy and rapport ... to sense how others think, make decisions and view the world.

Daniel Goleman's bestseller, Working with Emotional Intelligence, claims we reach our goals by managing our thoughts and feelings so that they are expressed appropriately and effectively. Following are the characteristics of emotional intelligence that Goleman identified.

"Wisdom is the power to put our time and our knowledge to the proper use."
Thomas J. Watson

Self Awareness
Knowing what we are feeling in the moment and using those preferences to guide our decision making; having a realistic assessment of our own abilities and a well-grounded sense of self-confidence.

Self Regulation
Handling our emotions so that they facilitate rather than interfere with the task at hand; being conscientious and delaying gratification to pursue goals; recovering well from emotional distress.

Motivation
Using our deepest preferences to move and guide us toward our goals, to help us take initiative and strive to improve; to persevere in the face of setbacks.

Empathy
Sensing what other people are feeling, being able to take their perspective, and cultivating rapport and attunement with a broad diversity of people.

Social Skills
Handling emotions in relationships well, and accurately reading social situations; interacting smoothly; using these skills to persuade, lead, negotiate and settle disputes, for cooperation and teamwork.

Napoleon Hill is considered by many to be the father of the personal development movement. Hill spent 20 years studying the world's most successful individuals, interviewing over 500 of the world's business, political and spiritual leaders and uncovered these 17 universal principles of success and achievement:

Direction
Knowing what your goals are - knowing what you want - fills you with a success consciousness and protects you against failure.

Mastermind Principle
The coordination of effort between two or more people in a spirit of perfect harmony in order to attain a specific objective.

Applied Faith
A state of mind through which your aims, desires, plans and purposes are translated into their physical or financial equivalent.

Pleasing Personality
The ability to get along with other people.

Going The Extra Mile
Rendering more and better service than you are paid to render, doing it all the time and doing it with a pleasing, positive attitude.

Self-Discipline
The ability to control our thoughts and emotions, self-discipline is the only thing in life over which you have complete, unchallenged and unchallengeable control.

Controlled Attention
The act of coordinating all your mind's faculties and directing their combined power to a given end.

Enthusiasm
A contagious state of mind that not only helps you gain the cooperation of

others but, more importantly, inspires you to draw upon and use the power of your imagination.

Imagination
The ability to reassemble old ideas and established facts into new combinations and put them to new uses.

Learning from Adversity
Having the insight and patience to learn the important messages from hardship, and setbacks.

Budgeting Time and Money
Knowing yourself and your habits, and having discipline around these two most vital factors.

Positive Mental Attitude
Governing your mind so that you might govern your life. The ability to see the seeds of a benefit in every single setback.

Accurate Thinking
Recognizing all the facts of life, both good and bad, assuming responsibility for separating and organizing the two, choosing which serves your needs and rejecting all others.

Good Health
A sense of well-being within body, mind and soul, and everything in moderation.

Cooperation
The willing cooperation and coordination of effort to achieve a specific objective.

Cosmic Habitforce
Understanding the power of the universe to manifest that which we think of on a habitual basis.

Achievement Drive

"Every man has two educations - that which is given him and the other which he gives himself. What we are merely taught seldom nourishes the mind like that which we teach ourselves. Indeed, all that is most worthy in a man he must work out and conquer for himself."

Jean Paul Richer

In addition to acceptance of 100% responsibility and self-control, the most critical attitudinal factor in your ability to manage time is achievement drive.

Achievement drive gives us our desire for results, our driving ambition to meet objectives and standards. People with high achievement drive set challenging goals and take calculated risks. They relentlessly pursue information that will reduce uncertainty and help them find ways to do things better. They are constantly learning how to improve their performance.

High achievers demand a lot of themselves and of others, with a core value of always doing better than they did before. It's an enormous personal challenge, but those with achievement drive live it and love it, as long as they take the time to 'smell the roses' along the way.

"The man who is too old to learn was probably always too old to learn."
Henry S. Hasskins

Managing yourself to success demands a balanced drive to achieve. Studies that compare 'star' performers to 'average' ones in executive ranks find the single strongest competence that sets apart 'star' from 'average' executives is the need to achieve.

Track your success

Those driven by the need to achieve seek ways to track their success. For many this means money - though they often say that money is a less important commodity than feedback on how well they are doing. Even those with moderate levels of achievement rely on performance measures. They may create their own measures for performance, setting goals like outperforming peers, doing a job more quickly, spending more time doing and less time in meetings, or beating some competitor.

Get Feedback

But for many people, getting performance feedback can be frustratingly difficult because of the immeasurable nature of their work. Such people have to develop a strong sense of where they are, in order to provide the feedback themselves. Top performers seek out the feedback they need at the point when it is most useful to them, and if they can't get it elsewhere, they give it to themselves

Control your Attitude

There is a saying in India, "When a pickpocket meets a saint, all he sees are the pockets." Our attitudes shape how we see the world; our attention is selective, and what matters most is what we automatically look for and see. Someone who is motivated by results notices the results he/she gets. They look for ways to do better, to be entrepreneurial, to innovate, or to find a competitive advantage.

Learning to Learn

The good news is that the requirements for achievement seem to be largely learned, and continue to develop as we go through life and learn from our experiences - our competence in achievement keeps growing. But competence cannot be developed by traditional means, not memorized or taught ... it is intensely mastered by individuals who are motivated to learn how create the life that they love.

You learn most thoroughly that which you want to learn. If you decide to learn how to manage your time, and if your word 'decide' contains plenty of 'desire and perseverance', you will most certainly be successful.

You are responsible for learning ... the coach, the teacher, the seminar leader, the books can only provide you with information. They can only facilitate your learning. You determine what you're going to do with the opportunity, and you haven't learned how to do anything until you can do it on your own.

"If you give a person a fish, he will eat once; if you teach him how to fish, he will eat the rest of his life."
Chinese proverb

History is full of self-taught people who have reached the pinnacle of success. Inspirational stories of men and women who overcame adversity because they were driven to learn and succeed. They wanted to learn.

The whole world opens up to those with a thirst for knowledge, the inquisitive ones, the curious, the persistent. When you enthusiastically accept responsibility for learning, you can learn anything!

You learn by asking

If you don't understand, or need to know more, it's your responsibility to ask the right questions.

45

You learn by being resourceful

If you want or need more, it's your responsibility to find out where it is and how to get it.

You learn by analyzing

It's your responsibility to analyze information and alternatives, determining what is practical, what will provide you with the greatest positive impact, and how to put it into action.

You learn by doing

It is your responsibility to immediately implement and practice useful ideas, adapting them to your circumstances and turning them into habits.

You learn by making mistakes

Don't expect perfection, and don't be afraid of messing up. It's up to you to be courageous ... just do it.

You learn by being open to new ideas

Don't pre-judge what you hear, read or see. Allow your mind to run free, to think beyond the common beliefs of society. You're responsible for seeing the possibility in everything.

"Learning is not attained by chance, it must be sought for with ardor and attended to with diligence."
Abigail Adams
1780

You learn by being persistent

If you don't learn it the first time, you're responsible for trying until you do.

You learn by being patient

Impatience closes the mind. You're responsible for maintaining inner calm, realizing that there is an order to it all, and not trying to run before you walk.

You learn by listening and concentrating

You have to be completely present to the moment in order to appreciate any learning opportunity. You're responsible for eliminating, or ignoring all distractions.

You learn through faith and confidence

When you believe it, you'll see it. You're responsible for developing and maintaining the belief.

You learn when you're committed

Until one is committed, there is hesitancy. You're responsible for making and keeping the commitment.

You learn when you are ready

When the student is ready, the teacher appears. You are responsible for knowing when you are ready, and for being open so that you recognize your teacher.

You learn from everything every day

Life has much to teach us. It is your responsibility to see the lesson in everyday things.

Self-Discipline

"The true basis of discipline is self-discipline, this embraces the idea of self-control and self-restraint and implies a life ordered by certain voluntarily imposed limitations; that duty comes before pleasure and these privileges are enjoyed only if responsibility and obligations are willingly shouldered."

William Mathews

Large doses of self-discipline are required to make your time management system work. It takes discipline to plan your day ... every day. It takes discipline to stick with one important job until it's finished, to keep working when friends and colleagues drop by. It takes discipline to apply the techniques covered in this program, to eliminate procrastination, to have integrity in the moment of decision. It takes discipline not to answer every phone call, and to limit your time on the ones you have. It takes discipline to do what it takes, and not offend others.

"It is impossible for a man to be cheated by anyone but himself."
Ralph Waldo Emerson

Self-discipline is like a muscle

If your discipline is weak from lack of use then start working it slowly, building up its strength little by little. Practice your discipline, use your discipline muscle daily and eventually you'll be able to move mountains with its strength.

Poor health or fatigue undermines attempts at self-discipline

When you are not feeling your best you don't always have the mental and emotional energy to concentrate on the job at hand. You have to take care of yourself ... regular exercise, good eating habits, plenty of sleep and balance in your life.

Lack of interest.

Indifference is a powerful de-motivator. If you're bored or unchallenged, you will find it more difficult to exercise the discipline needed to work well. Examine your attitude toward your work, and honestly evaluate your situation. Is the problem with the work or with your place in it?

Laziness

Self-discipline is a habit, and lack of it is a habit too. Is this simply a case of old fashioned laziness? If you're typically lazy, re-affirm what your goals will do for you once you've achieved them. Look at pictures of what your goals are or mean. See yourself as already having achieved them, then go out and do what it takes to get there.

Lack of awareness or motivation

You've been relatively successful thus far, and never thought much about discipline. If you want to continue to get what you've always got - that's Okay. But if you want to create something more, something greater - it takes discipline to do more than you have done before.

Set up circumstances that provide positive reinforcement and recognize your self-discipline.

Keep your goals visible. Whenever you are tempted to procrastinate or dawdle, your goals will refocus you.

"For everything there is a season and a time for every matter under heaven. He has made everything beautiful under the sun."
Ecclesiastes 3:1,11

Use all available tools

Utilize your work planning system, telephone timer, goal picture book etc., to reinforce self-discipline.

Set deadlines

Even if the project doesn't have one. Even better, break it down into steps with deadlines for each. Nothing creates a sense of urgency and discipline like a deadline.

Plan your activities and establish priorities

Without this you will mentally wander around in a most undisciplined fashion.

Reward yourself

Success should not go unrewarded. When you complete a goal or even when you recognize that you were unnaturally disciplined, give yourself a reward. Treat yourself often and immediately after you earn it.

Pick a hero for a model

Our world is filled with stories about ordinary people who faced impossible challenges with strong will, and overcame them. Edison failed 1499 times to discover rubber; Helen Keller overcame deafness and blindness in an age when people were diagnosed incorrectly as mentally incompetent; Colonel Sanders wandered America for three years trying to sell his recipe. Find someone you respect and can relate to.

Act 'as if' you are already self-disciplined

Create the habit of self-discipline by acting as though you have it - soon you will! You'll be surprised how quickly habits form. Real achievement in developing powerful personal habits comes from attending patiently, persistently and intelligently to the process. Act as if you are disciplined, and you will become disciplined.

Attitude Exercises

Analyze Your Feelings

What are some of the things you have to implement in order for the Time and Self Management program to make a difference? What are some of the new habits you have to introduce? List them and indicate what word best describes how you honestly feel when you visualize having to implement each of these. (Sample feeling words include concerned, worried, expectant, joyful, distaste etc). For this exercise to work you must complete it before moving on to the next exercise.

Have To's   Feelings

_____   _____

_____   _____

_____   _____

_____   _____

_____   _____

_____   _____

_____   _____

Adjust Your Feelings, then Your Attitude will Follow

You don't have to do anything. There are only consequences or results from what you choose to do. Your world will not come to an end if you don't implement the ideas that come out of the Time and Self Management program. You may not be happy if you don't practice them, and there may be real consequences if you don't. That's understandable. The big point is that you don't have to.

Everything in life is a choice

All of the results you are currently experiencing in your life are absolutely perfect for you. This includes your career, personal relationships, and financial status. How could it be otherwise? The reason you are where you are in life, is simply a result of all the choices you have made to this point. The actions that contribute the most value, that last the longest, that have the most powerful influence over our lives, are actions that we choose to do because we want to, not because we have to.

Let's switch gears. Make a list of the new time and self management habits you want to implement. This is a different list. What are you really looking forward to doing .... what are you truly committed to doing. Indicate what you believe this will achieve for you, then indicate how you really feel about it.

Want To's	Achievements	Feelings

Things To Do
To Create an Effective Attitude

1. Believe that you can do anything you set your mind to.
2. Expect to do well and you will do well.
3. Look for the good in people and circumstance.
4. Accept complete responsibility for your emotions, and what you create.
5. Act consistent with your beliefs.
6. Stay aware of what you are thinking and feeling.
7. See the seed of a benefit in every adversity.
8. Act 'as if' you already have a positive attitude.
9. Look for the lessons in life.
10. Practice self-discipline.
11. Reward yourself when you deserve it.

"Second floor please"

chapter four

Self Management...

Stress Control

Responsibility and Emotional Control

"To be a man is, precisely, to be responsible. It is to feel shame at the sight of what seems to be unmerited misery. It is to take pride in victory won by one's comrades. It is to feel, when setting one's stone, that one is contributing to the building of the world."

Antoine de Saint Exupery

Accept 100% responsibility

We are 100% responsible for our lives, and acceptance of this responsibility, without excuses, is a true hallmark of peak performing, high achieving, self-actualized human beings.

Nobody else can accept, change or create what we have in this world. Nobody else can institute time saving habits, or eliminate time wasters. Nothing else determines our ecstasy or our despair.

It is easy to blame others for our failures, for our moods and our losses ... to make excuses for the way we are, for the way we feel, for what we do. Accepting full responsibility, no matter the circumstances, is the difference between personal power or weakness.

The more fully we accept responsibility, the more control we have over our time, our lives, our emotions, our happiness and our success.

Control your state of mind

The ultimate act of personal responsibility may be in taking control of our own state of mind. Moods exert a powerful pull on thought, memory and perception. When we are angry, our thoughts become preoccupied with the object of our anger, and irritability so skews our view that an otherwise harmless comment might appear hostile. Resisting this destructive quality of moods is essential to our ability to work productively, to make the best use of our time.

Control your negative emotions

The most difficult responsibility for most people to accept is that of their destructive emotions. They refuse to acknowledge that emotions are within their control, that they create them and that they're responsible for them.

Trying to drive your life in the face of negative emotions is like trying to drive your car with the emergency brake on. You can move forward, but not very quickly, and it puts stress on the system. Negative emotions wear us out and sap our energy.

Manage your stress

> *"To succeed it is necessary to accept the world as it is and rise above it."*
> Michael Korda

People best able to handle distress often have a stress management technique they call upon when needed, whether it's a long bath, a workout, yoga, a walk in the park, or meditation. Regular daily practice of a relaxation method seems to reset the mental trigger points, making you less easily provoked. In a relaxed state, we can more accurately monitor our emotional upsets, and recover from distress sooner.

Choose your meanings and interpretations

You can control your negative emotions ... they reflect your interpretations and your reactions to various situations. Something happens and you interpret it; you give it meaning. You make it mean one thing and I can make it mean something completely different. These interpretations and meanings instantaneously affect our emotions.

Nothing gives us our interpretations and meanings, we choose them. Accepting responsibility gives us the power to choose and ultimately create the emotions we want.

Stop blaming

One of the control points of negative emotions is blame. Blaming others is a way out, a way of avoiding responsibility for the way we are or feel. Blaming ourselves results in destructive self-criticism and guilt, and does not generate positive action. The instant we stop assigning blame, our negative emotions stop. Being responsible, and acting out of that responsibility in a positive constructive fashion, enables us to build the future we want.

You can stop blaming ... every single time something happens that causes you to feel angry or upset, immediately replace the blame thought with: "I am responsible for what I do with this situation". The conscious mind can only hold one thought at a time, and it will become a positive one.

Control yourself

Something happens and you get angry. It's a natural and quick reaction that you didn't even have time to think about. Feeling anger, frustration, disappointment, are all natural. But you don't have to let the feelings control your actions. Take responsibility, ride out the adrenaline rush with a few deep breaths. If you can't handle the situation right now, walk away until you can. Then do or say the right thing instead of the quick, reactive thing that your emotions determine.

Ultimately you are responsible for the effect your emotion creates in the world and you can control it.

"The emphasis in sound discipline must be on what's wrong, rather than who's to blame."
George S Odiorne

Stress Control

More than anything, it's the stress we allow ourselves to feel that negatively impacts our ability to focus. Try these stress reduction techniques to improve your power of concentration:

Change your viewpoint
View rudeness or sarcasm as a reflection of the speaker.

Put your problems into perspective
Few problems are actually catastrophic. Break big problems into smaller ones and solve one at a time. Be optimistic; learn from your mistakes. If you get lemons, make lemonade. Laugh at life. See the glass half full, or even better, see the miracle in a single drop of water.

"When faced with the choice of changing one's mind, or proving there is no need to, almost everybody gets busy with the proof".
John Kenneth Galbraith

Stop worrying, start working
'Worry' comes from the Anglo-Saxon word meaning to strangle or choke, and it prevents you from thinking or acting effectively. Stop fretting and take action ... work towards changing the situation you find intolerable. If you can do anything, then do it. If there is nothing to be done, then stop wasting your time and energy worrying about it. Choose not to worry.

Stop talking yourself down.
Look at your accomplishments, take pride in what you have or have done. Utilize reminders of your personal strength and ability to reach your goals. When you do well, congratulate yourself.

Slow down your life
Take time to smell the roses. Living a life in the fast lane burns more gas and requires more stops to refuel. Choose a hobby that can't be rushed like painting, gardening or playing a musical instrument . Take a slow walk through nature, noticing everything. Listen to the birds. Practice yoga or meditation. Increasingly, stressed executives are discovering that the powers of Eastern philosophy can offer genuine benefits in the world of business. By calming your body and mind, you not only reduce stress, but make it easier to solve problems and reach decisions. Leave your work behind.

Remember to breathe
When we become stressed, our breathing gets faster and more shallow, only

the upper portions of our lungs are used. Oxygen does not get to the outer regions of our brain and body, causing an inability to concentrate. Stop and take several deep, even breaths once every hour (be careful not to turn them into sighs, which might reinforce any frustration you're feeling) and you'll find yourself energized and ready to tackle new challenges.

Treat your body

Treat yourself to a therapeutic massage, chiropractor, sauna, whirlpool, vitamin and mineral supplements. Drink lots of water, it cleans out your internal systems. Get enough sleep each night, and if you're feeling tired during the day don't be afraid to take a little cat-nap ... you'll make up for lost time with increased energy and concentration.

Exercise regularly

Moderate, regular exercise that increases your heart rate and requires concentration serves two purposes: it takes your mind away from work and other pressures, and it strengthens your heart, allowing it to work under stress with less effort. Stretching for 15 minutes each day will increase your flexibility and ward off aches, pains and muscle degeneration.

Eat Right

Protein and carbohydrates for breakfast keep energy levels high all morning. Sugar produces a rapid burst of energy, but slowly decreases blood glucose, resulting in loss of energy and concentration. Heavy lunches divert blood to the digestive system reducing mental stamina. Read food labels. Saturated fats and hydrogenated oils are extremely bad for you. Don't eat after 9:00 p.m. as your food will not get digested properly ... it puts a strain on your digestive system, distracting you from a good nights sleep while increasing your body fat.

"Life is what happens while you are making other plans."
John Lennon

Focus, Concentration and Enjoying Each Moment

Effective time and self management requires absolute focus and concentration. You must be diligent in applying the techniques and systems that move you closer to achieving peak performance, and towards the important goals you've set for yourself.

Focus and concentration allow you to tackle both menial and critical tasks with single-minded purpose ... to stay on purpose, overcoming a variety of obstacles to their conclusion ... and it's developed by practicing complete, unbreakable attention to whatever concerns you.

Clear the mind

Look at a calculator ... you have to hit the Clear button and either store to Memory, or completely clear away one problem, before you employ it to solve another.

All too often we try to use our minds to work on several problems at once without ever stopping to hit the Clear button. Achieving maximum personal productivity requires that you become extremely adept at stopping, storing and clearing in order to direct 100% of your mental powers to one matter at a time, to the matter at hand. You need to control your thoughts and manage your mind and focus your attention in order to control or manage time.

If you have difficulty moving adeptly and completely from one task to another, try adapting a 'clearing technique' such as closing your eyes and taking several deep breaths, counting to ten, or just concentrating on your breathing for a few moments. It could even be as simple as just telling yourself not to be distracted, and moving on to the next task immediately.

"Go as far as you can see, and when you get there you'll see farther."
Anonymous

How to Enjoy Each Moment

The by-product of improving management of time is that it gives you more control over your life. You enjoy more of your life when you have a system that allows you to choose what you do with your time.

You enjoy each moment, as you naturally become more present to what you are doing while you're doing it ... this inherent benefit occurs for virtually everyone who improves their time and self management.

Flow

Creating Flow

Flow is a natural state in the universe that allows us to expend less effort and get more results. There are things in our lives that clog up the potential for flow according to effectiveness expert Ed Strachar. You can assist in the creation of flow in your work and in your life by following these techniques as he outlined in his work "Into the Genius Zone"

Eliminate the clutter in your life
Clean out your closets, garage, office and everything else that is a mess. Clutter clogs up flow

Resolve Conflicts
Clean up any unresolved conflicts with your friends, family, coworkers or acquaintances through prayer, letters, apologies, phone calls or forgiveness. How long are you going to let that incident three years ago affect you? Unresolved conflicts clog up flow.

Express your feelings and attitudes
Get in touch with how you feel and what you think, and express it with tact and diplomacy. Unexpressed feelings and attitudes clog up flow.

Live up to your agreements
If you say you're going to do something, then do it. If you agree to be somewhere at a certain time, then be on time. If you promise yourself something, honour the promise. Incomplete agreements clog up flow.

Complete Tasks
Don't start things and leave them undone like frayed tassels at the end of a rope. If you start something then finish it ... and that includes the clean-up and paperwork. Incomplete tasks clog up flow.

Hold your vision
Keep your vision or purpose top of mind. It can act like a beacon, keeping you in flow through the daily storms. Lack of vision clogs up flow.

> *"Wherever you go, go with your whole heart"*
> Confucius

Use your brilliance to help others
If you are good at something, share it for the good of others. Selfishness clogs flow.

Flow and Achievement

"Believing is one thing, doing another. Many talk like the sea but their lives are stagnant marshes. Still others raise their heads above the mountain tops, while their souls cling to the dark walls of caves."

Kahlil Gibran

High achievers find their work exhilarating - and perform at their best. The key to that exhilaration is not the task itself - it can often be quite routine - but the special state of mind they create as they work, a state called 'flow'. Flow moves people to do their best work, no matter what work they do.

Be completely present to what you are doing

Flow blossoms when our skills and attention are fully engaged by a work project that stretches us in new and challenging ways. The challenge absorbs us so much that we lose ourselves in our work, becoming so totally engaged that we may feel 'time stand still'. In this state we seem to handle everything effortlessly, nimbly adapting to shifting demands. Flow itself is a pleasure.

Star performers are 'present to the moment' while working. They are emotionally present at work. When people are present in this sense, they are fully attentive and completely involved in their work - and so perform at their best. They eliminate distractions and concentrate completely on what they are doing 'right now'.

In communication, being present requires 'not being distracted by other thoughts, and so being open to others rather than closed'. When fully present, we become aware of the needs and emotions of those around us, and can adapt to what is needed. We can be thoughtful, funny, or self-reflective, drawing on whatever capacity or skill we need at the moment. We are ultimately 'in flow'.

There is flow in work you love

"The real voyage of discovery consists not in making new landscapes but in having new eyes."
Marcel Proust

Motive and emotion share the same Latin root, motere, 'to move'. Emotions are, literally, what moves us to pursue our goals; they shape our perceptions and drive our actions. Great work starts with a great feeling, and great feelings about work help to create flow.

For top performers, flow and task are intimately connected; flow occurs in the work that is most critical to their goals and productivity, rather than in fascinating diversions or distractions. For high achievers, excellence and pleasure in work are one and the same.

Flow is the ultimate motivator. Activities we love draw us in because we get into flow as we pursue them. Of course, what gives people such pleasure varies immensely. Take a close look at what you love to do ... the actions and activities that generate value for your employer. This is where your greatness lies.

Look again at the areas of work you identified in your Personal Profile Summary at the beginning of the workbook. Do what it takes now to focus your efforts on these areas. Spend more time doing what you love, create flow and achieve outstanding results.

On-a-Roll and Visualization

Being 'On a Roll'

There are days, or times, when everything works - opportunities abound, doors swing open easily, recognition occurs, several sales you've been working on all come to fruition at once. If you're accustomed to only a few new client prospects or opportunities developing in a week, you'll be flooded with dozens instead.

When this phenomenon occurs, feel the flow and concentrate on doing more.

The feeling that everything is going right gives you stratospheric confidence ... make the contacts you've been avoiding, make that proposal, negotiate for something you believe in. Stay a little later, stop and make a sales call on the way home. This isn't the time to take it easy, it's time to go full out.

It's vitally important during these times to be on guard against anybody or anything that may snuff out the fire. When you're on a roll, its like the universe is there for you ... don't let negative thinkers and time wasters distract you.

How to attract the roll

It happens when you least expect it, but when it does, it's because you deserve it. It seems to happen to action-driven people, to those already in pursuit of worthwhile, well defined goals; it occurs to those who associate with other peak performers; it often starts with a single 'big break' which you're astute enough to recognize and exploit. Have faith, act with confidence, follow your passion and look for the good in people and circumstance.

> *"It is the spirit of the quest which determines its outcome."*
> Indian Proverb

Visualization

Visualization is the act of the imagination by which you form clear mental images ... seeing something in the mind's eye. Visualization is a mental rehearsal, the living of an experience in advance of it really happening. It provides you with the phenomenal ability to see, and ultimately affect the outcome of your actions.

You perform better each time you do something ... practice makes perfect. The power of visualization allows you to practice something in your mind, enhancing proper preparation to generate outstanding results.

Visualization dramatically increases performance, and the effectiveness of your actions. It's a powerful tool used by some of the world's most successful athletes, entertainers, leaders, and salespeople. It's simple to master, but one of the most under-utilized achievement techniques available to mankind.

Relationship Building

Your discipline must also transcend into the area of human relations. You must acknowledge the importance of people, not just tasks, in order to be fully self-actualized.

It is natural for persistent, time-conscious, list driven achievers with a sense of urgency to verbally swat aside anyone who delays them from knocking things off their list. Equally important to accomplishing the tasks on your list is the discipline to develop outstanding human relationships. The quality of our lives is directly related to the quality of the relationships we have with others.

Here once again, the universal law applies ... everything we do comes back to us. We achieve joy in our lives not by looking for joy, but by bringing joy to others; we impress others by being impressed with them; we gain trust by trusting others; we gain respect by showing respect to others. If you want outstanding relationships, be an outstanding human being ... it's as simple as that.

Your ability to treat everyone equally, to get along with the greatest number of people ... whether rich or poor, minority or majority, young or old, indicates high levels of self-esteem and catapults you to peak performance. The quality of our relationships depends solely on how important we make others feel. Here's how you can make others feel important.

Raise their self-esteem

Do everything possible to make others feel good about themselves ... to feel good about their decisions, their accomplishments, their efforts and their being. Be sincere and be specific.

Accept them

Acceptance is one of the deepest cravings of the human spirit. Accept people for who they are and who they aren't. Smile at others when you see them, accept them unconditionally, without judgement.

Express sincere appreciation and gratitude

Look for opportunities to say Thank You, and be specific about what you are thanking them for.

Express admiration

Recognize and publicly admire positive traits such as punctuality, generosity, kindness, sincerity, etc. Be sincere and be specific.

Accept responsibility

If you've made a mistake, if you've hurt someone, accept the responsibility and apologize. Contrary to what many people think, nobody knows you're sorry unless you say it. Apologizing is not a sign of weakness, it's a sign of self-esteem. Ultimately, we are responsible for all that our actions, words and moods create in the world. Give yourself permission to be wrong!

Never criticize

Nothing destroys human spirit, undermines self-esteem, lowers self-confidence and causes negative reactions more than destructive criticism. Don't criticize, even in jest.

Build Rapport

The fastest way to build rapport with another individual is to be just like them. Look for things you have in common, or mirror their body language.

Avoid Arguments

When we argue with others, we're indicating that their thoughts, opinions and values are wrong. Given the choice to be right or to be kind, always choose kind. If you absolutely, positively have to point out that someone is clearly wrong, use the 'straw man' technique ..."What would you say to someone who disagrees with you because of (_____)?"

Be genuine, courteous and sincere

Care about people, wish them the best, ask about their children, show courtesy, open doors, don't sit down until your guest is seated; be patient and polite.

Pay attention to people - Listen to them

Nothing builds relationships or makes people feel important, as quickly and as solidly, as paying attention to them. This means listening. Listening intently builds trust, rapport, and strong friendships. Concentrate completely on what the other person is saying. Eliminate distractions. When your mind wanders, bring your attention back to the speaker. Practice the powerful listening skills outlined in the next module.

"The most important single ingredient in the formula of success is knowing how to get along with people."
Theodore Roosevelt

Stress Exercises

Dr. David Lewis' 60 Second Stress Test

Dr. David Lewis in his book, '10 minute Time and Stress Management', describes the symptoms of 'hurry sickness':
• Never having enough time in the day to meet all the demands made on you.
• Feeling angry and frustrated by delays, however unavoidable.
• Attempting to do everything too quickly.
• Difficulty winding down once you arrive home.
• Inability to relax even on holiday.
• Lack of patience when dealing with people slower-paced than yourself.
• Leaving things to the last minute.
• Needing a 'deadline high' to motivate you.

Are you a victim of hurry sickness? Take this 60 second test and find out.

Without looking at your watch, or silently counting seconds, estimate the passing of one minute. When you think time is up, check how much has actually elapsed

What your result reveals:

• Less than 55 seconds. You are a victim of 'hurry sickness', and the less time that elapsed the more serious your condition. But don't be too concerned. There are practical procedures to help reduce that needless stress my managing your time more effectively.

• Between 55 and 65 seconds. Although you do not, generally, suffer from 'hurry sickness' you may still find there are too few hours each day to accomplish all you want or need to achieve. If so, utilize practical procedures to help you gain greater control of your life.

• More than 66 seconds. You have a relaxed attitude to the passing of time, and dislike having to race against the clock. The greater the lapsed time, the less likely you are to suffer from the symptoms of 'hurry sickness'.
It is important to understand that 'hurry sickness' is bad for you, but equally important to understand that stress can be good for you. When used correctly, stress releases hidden reserves of creative energy, enabling you to produce at peak performance and enjoy a happier, healthier and even more fulfilling life. The goal is not to eliminate stress, but to understand it, what creates it, control its effect on us and use it to our advantage.

The Saintly Relationship Challenge

None of us are perfect, in fact there are even recorded faults attributed to Jesus Christ and Buddha. So don't be too hard on yourself when completing this exercise. The objective is to accept responsibility for who you are in your transactions with others, and strive to honour them. This doesn't mean you allow others to completely disrespect you or your time. What it means is that you communicate sincerely, with courtesy, and without judgment. Even the smallest steps to improve the way you communicate will bring you more satisfaction, raise your self-esteem and in the end bring you closer to achieving what you want out of life.

Step 1

Think of someone you find annoying and describe how you would rate your contribution to communication with them (on a scale of 1-10) in the following areas;

Raising their self-esteem . . . . _____

Acceptance of them for who they are . . . . _____

Admiration of them . . . . _____

Accepting responsibility for how you make them feel . . . . . _____

Withholding criticism . . . . _____

Courtesy . . . . _____

Sincerity . . . . _____

Concentrating on listening to them . . . . _____

Step 2

Review the above areas and be clear in your mind what they mean. Think of what you could say or do that would improve the scores. Think of how you would do it sincerely.

Step 3

Search this individual out when they appear to be able to talk. Tell them you haven't had much of a chance to chat (or something like that) and find out any or all of the following: Where they grew up, their children's interests, what they like to do in their spare time, what they did last weekend, what they are most proud of having accomplished. Be absolutely sincere in your communication ... don't interrogate them - be interested in them. Take 10-15 minutes to increase your rapport and relationship with this individual. When it's time to move on, thank them for taking the time to chat and that it was nice getting to know them a little bit. Then politely excuse yourself so that you can get working on the project.

Step 4
How would you rate your contribution to communication after this interaction (1-10)
Raising their self-esteem .... ———
Acceptance of them for who they are .... ———
Admiration of them .... ———
Accepting responsibility for how you make them feel ..... ———
Withholding criticism .... ———
Courtesy .... ———
Sincerity .... ———
Concentrating on listening to them .... ———

Step 5
Cherish and appreciate what you have just accomplished. Determine what areas came the easiest for you, and embrace them. What did you have the most difficulty with; are these consistent throughout many of your interactions; can you commit to reducing their impact on your relationships.

A simple visualization exercise

• Before going into any key interaction, be it with a boss, co-worker or client, find a place where you can be alone. Allow yourself 15 or 20 minutes, sit down quietly and close your eyes.

• Take a few deep breaths and think only of your breathing. If you find yourself thinking of something else, simply notice the thought and bring your attention back to your breathing.

• Count backwards from 30, counting with every breath you take. Every time you notice your thoughts wander away from the countdown, simply notice those thoughts, then return to your countdown.

• Begin to picture yourself in this interaction: where it takes place, how you enter the room, see what you're wearing, what the greeting will be like.

• Notice how you feel, your mood, your attitude. When your thoughts drift away, gently notice them, then return to your visualization.

• Play through the conversation as you think it will occur. Allow your mind to run free, to assume what will happen and what will be said. See it from beginning to end.

• Now start again at the beginning ... use the power of your mind to change the picture ... visualize the situation the way you want it to be. Be present to each moment as it unfolds.

• How do you want to feel ... play through the interaction and feel it; what do you want to say ... play through the interaction and say it; who do you want to be ... determine to be that person and see yourself in the interaction as that person.

• Be in control of your thoughts, your emotions and your reactions. Picture the worst possible thing happening, and how you handle it with confidence. Then play through the entire interaction as you want it to occur, right up to its successful conclusion.

• Each time you notice your mind wandering, simply notice the thought ... don't get frustrated, don't try to push out the distracting thought ... simply take notice of it and come back to your visualization.

• When you're ready to return to reality, slowly picture where you are, move your fingers, shrug your shoulders, take a few deep breaths, and slowly open your eyes. You will find yourself calm, confident and effective as you move into virtually any interaction.

Things To Do
to Control Your Stress

1. Practice Mindfulness, become consistently aware of your thoughts and emotions.
2. Take complete responsibility, stop blaming people and circumstance for your stress.
3. Choose the meaning you give to things.
4. Meditate daily.
5. Choose not to let stress adversely affect you.
6. Develop patience.
7. Give yourself a 'time out' ... take a walk, think only of your surroundings and calm down.
8. Stop worrying, take action or forget about it.
9. Take time to smell the roses, appreciate what you have in comparison to those that have nothing.
10. Treat your body like a temple; eat, sleep and exercise properly.
11. Remember to breathe.
12. Become present to each moment, get into flow.
13. Do work that you love.
14. Practice visualization.
15. Build relationships, become other-conscious.
16. Concentrate completely on what you are doing, while you are doing it.
17. Spend time in nature.

"Any luck?"

chapter five

Self Management...

Direction

The Importance of Goals

"A person has to be working toward an end or he will find himself weaving baskets. You can't live in a vacuum or as a dot surrounded by infinity. You have to have a goal, and a time limit for getting there."

Edward Streeter

The greatest waste of time in our lives is action that does not bring us closer to achieving the important things in our lives. There are thousands of activities that call out for our time every day, and it's critical that we understand which of these activities are worthwhile. As such, the starting point of any effective time management program is to establish clear, specific, meaningful goals. Goals allow us to concentrate our efforts on the important things, and enable us to effectively prioritize and deal with various demands on our time. They are the root of our daily plan which makes time our partner, not our enemy. They are our terms of reference when faced with making decisions on what to spend our valuable time on.

Goals are simply dreams you take action on. They're something that you want, and are willing to work to achieve. They involve the ongoing pursuit of a worthy objective until accomplished.

The idea of goals probably makes you somewhat uncomfortable - you probably associate them with New Year's resolutions. You make them because you think you should, but sooner or later your efforts fall off. You're not alone. Research suggests that as few as 3% of the population set goals. These are, however, the peak performers who actively take control of their lives, initiate positive change and out-perform their peers by more than 10 times.

Goal setting is non-negotiable for successful time management. You can choose to succeed or you can choose to drift; clearly defined goals will help keep you steering in the right direction.

Goals are indispensable to:
1. Focus your efforts
2. Clarify your thoughts
3. Assist in establishing priorities
4. Improve motivation
5. Encourage and recognize achievement

"A man of knowledge lives by acting, not by thinking about acting ... Thus a man of knowledge sweats and puffs and if one looks at him he is just like an ordinary man, except that the folly of his life is under his control"
Carlos Castenada

Have a balance of goals
Avoid focusing too narrowly on one aspect of your life at the expense of others. If you had your life to live over again, what would you give a higher priority to? How do you want to be remembered?

A balanced life with goals and achievements in various areas leads to more complete self-fulfillment, and allows you to be more productive everywhere. Ask yourself what you would like to be, have, do, learn, become, or experience in each of the areas listed below. What part of your life are you missing out on?

Relationship Goals
What do you want for the pleasure of your loved ones?
Business and career goals
What positions, earnings, accomplishments, recognition and awards would you like?
Personal goals
What would you like to learn, experience, and ultimately become for yourself?

Focus on one at a time
It is important to pick one goal in each of these areas that is abundantly more important than all the others, the accomplishment of which will lead to the attainment of many

other minor goals. When we try to accomplish too many things simultaneously, we find that our efforts are spread too thin, and in the end we accomplish nothing.

Achieve one critical goal then it will become relatively simple for you to set and achieve many more. The enclosed Goal Priority Draw exercises originally developed by Kevin W. McCarthy in his book, The On-Purpose Person, will help you establish your top priority goals.

"People are always blaming their circumstances for what they are. I don't believe in circumstance. The people who get on in this world are the people who get up and look for the circumstances they want, and if they can't find them, they make them."
George Bernard Shaw

Goal Setting Checklist

"Know how to arrange your life with discretion and not as accident may determine, but with foresight and choice. A wise man does at once what a fool does at last."

                                                        Baltasar Gracian

"Life is always opening new and unexpected things to us. There is no monotony in living to him who walks even the quietest and tamest path with open and perceiving eyes. The monotony of life, if life is monotonous to you, is in you, not in the world."

                                                        Phillip Brooks

There are several critical factors that must exist for the achievement of our goals. Here's a checklist that you can use as building blocks to set yours. Pick and choose the ones you're most comfortable with, but take note, the more aligned you are with all of these, the greater your chances of success.

You must really want it

Think about what it is that you really, really want ... these are the things that inherently carry the seeds of desire, and desire is the great motivator that propels us. These are truly the things that qualify as goals. Unless you really sincerely desire to be, do, or have something different, no technique or system in any book will empower you to reach them...

"When the dreams end there is no more greatness."
Hal Borland

You must really believe you can do it

Your goals must be realistically achievable ... within your area of power and responsibility, and where you have access to all the necessary resources. The more absolute belief you have in your ability to accomplish your goal, the more rapidly you will get there. The more realistic your goals, the more believable they become. If your goals are unrealistically high, you'll only frustrate yourself and give up. It has been proven time and again that lack of faith in your ability to reach goals will short-circuit success faster than any external factor possibly could.

Your goals must be specific and measurable

Be specific ... accurately define what you want. Your goals must be measurable, with identifiable steps that give you the ability to see your progress step by step. If your goal is vague, how will you know when you've reached it? One rule of thumb is that others should be able to determine, without conjecture, that you've reached it. Keep telling yourself to be more specific until it is crystal clear and measurable without a doubt.

Your goals must have deadlines

Deadlines perform a critical function in goal setting, providing a sense of urgency and a way to track progress, both of which increase the probability that a goal will be achieved. A goal without a deadline is more like a dream or a hope ... something you don't act on or consciously, proactively move towards.

Your goals must be challenging

Demanding goals create excitement, motivate you and give you an edge that prevents boredom. They must make you stretch, challenging you to work and be different than you normally would. Goals that force you to move out of your comfort zone teach you more about life and your capacity to succeed as you overcome more and greater obstacles. The more challenging your goals, the greater the joy and fulfillment once you reach them.

Your goals must be meaningful

They must mean enough that you will overcome adversity to achieve them. Ask yourself, "What's really important to me? What's the purpose of doing this? What am I prepared to do to get this?" If the goal is not truly yours, or if it doesn't get your adrenaline pumping, it probably has little meaning for you. Goals that mean more to your wife, spouse, boss or partner aren't really your goals and should be left out of this exercise.

"Ah, but a man's reach should exceed his grasp - or what's a heaven for?"
Robert Browning

Your goals must align with your values

Synergy and Flow are two words that describe any process moving effortlessly forward to completion. When your goals are in sync with your core values, the harmony makes decision-making easy, and creates an energy surge that propels you to much higher levels of success.

Your goals must be flexible

Don't lower your goals too quickly, but don't cling stubbornly to something that is no longer possible. You don't want to be so rigid that you feel suffocated or de-motivated. Flexible goals allow you the freedom to change course if a genuine opportunity comes along that is so good you'd be crazy not to pursue it.

Developing Your Plan to Achieve Goals

"The miracle power that elevates the few is to be found in their industry, application and perseverance, under the promptings of a brave determined spirit."

Mark Twain

You will never achieve big results in life without consistent and persistent action. Your action starts with industriously applying this planning process, and persevering until it's done.

By setting and achieving goals you are building the life you desire, and every builder needs a blueprint, a plan. This is a proven process for developing your plan. If you seriously want to achieve the goals you have set for yourself, you need to create a plan to achieve them. It doesn't need to be complicated ... simply follow the process, write out the steps you identify.

Following is a checklist derived from Brian Tracy's 'Psychology of Achievement' with an explanation of each step. Familiarize yourself with each step then complete the worksheet in the exercises at the end of this chapter. Use the worksheet to write it all down. You can't follow a plan that is only in your mind! The more order you put into it, the easier it will be to follow, and the more success you will realize.

1. Write your goal out in full

"Our duty is to proceed as if limits to our ability did not exist."
Pierre Teilhard de Chardin

Describe in complete detail what your goal looks like, exactly as you wish to have it, and by when. It is only a wish until it is committed to paper. Writing things down embeds them in your mind and makes them more real. Write out your goal according to the enclosed checklist.

2. Describe what it will do for you

List as many benefits, bi-products and advantages you will enjoy when you accomplish this goal. What will it allow you to do, what will it feel like when you achieve it?

3. Analyze your current status

Where are you now? Exactly what do you have now that provides a starting point for achieving this goal?

4. Identify the obstacles

Nothing of any significance in our lives is accomplished without having to overcome adversity. All great achievements require persistence and dogged determination in reacting positively to the things that get in our way. Write down all of the obstacles you can think of and you'll find they become smaller and less overwhelming. Getting them out of your mind and onto paper will free you up to creatively overcome them.

5.Identify the knowledge you will require

What do you have to learn that you don't know now, where and how can you learn it?

6. Identify people, groups, organizations who can help

The fastest way to get something, even the most outrageous request, is to simply ask for it. Determine who you should ask! Ask with confidence and courtesy, identify the reasons for your request, be thankful for cooperation but don't be offended if you're refused.

Selectively share your dreams with a few people you trust. Carefully choose proactive individuals who will support and encourage you when the going gets tough.

The nature of the universe is such that everything we do comes back to us over time. Our kindnesses are returned, as are our indiscretions. This universal law is a powerful force that comes into play in gaining the support of those whose assistance you require to reach your goals.

The starting point of all riches and success is to concentrate on what you can give, how you can serve, how you can contribute, how you can compensate and reward others. Do it gladly, willingly, and derive pleasure from it ... do not resent it. Take personal, private pride in giving, and if it's recognized, simply restate the pleasure it brings you. Always do more than people expect, or that you're paid to do. Under-promise and over-deliver. However, be careful to ensure that your kindness is authentic. It is only our genuine actions, with nothing expected in return, that generate genuine returns.

> *"Doest thou love life? Then do not squander time, for that is the stuff life is made of."*
> Benjamin Franklin

7. Make your plan

Take all of the details you've identified throughout this process and make a plan. Make it complete in every detail, listing the action steps you will take, and when they will be completed. Itemize the action steps by priority and by time. Break larger tasks down into smaller steps you can accomplish one at a time.The effort you put into this step will make everything else that follows easier, and further ensure that you will be prepared for what it will take to achieve the results you want.

8. Create a Picture Goals Book

To improve the focus and clarity of your goals, create a picture book that shows you what achieving these goals looks like. Use magazine clippings, photographs, etc. to represent what the achievement of each goal looks like.

9. Visualize your goals
The mind thinks in pictures, not words, and as we vividly picture in our minds what we desire, it will become reality. Look at your picture book daily. Close your eyes and visualize yourself already having achieved it. The sharper these images are and the more intense you feel, the more likely you are to create the desired result. This is a powerful process that should not be discounted.

Goal Commitment and Action

"Until one is committed, there is hesitancy, the chance to draw back, always ineffectiveness. Concerning all acts of initiative there is one elementary truth - the ignorance of which kills countless ideas and splendid plans ... that the moment when one definitely commits oneself, then Providence moves too. All sorts of things occur to help one that never otherwise would have occurred. A whole stream of events issues from the decision, raising in one's favour all manner of unforeseen incidents, meetings and material assistance, which no man could have dreamed would have come his way".

W.H. Murray
Scottish Himalayan Expedition

"The quality of persistence is to the character of man as carbon is to steel".
Napoleon Hill

"Do not pray for easy times; pray to be stronger men. Do not pray for tasks equal to your powers; pray for powers equal to your tasks."

John F. Kennedy

"When the morning's freshness has been replaced by the weariness of midday, when the leg muscles quiver under the strain, the climb seems endless, and, suddenly, nothing will go quite as you wish - it is then that you must not hesitate."

Dag Hammerskjold

"The journey of a thousand miles begins with one step."

Lao-Tzu

Just Do It
The best plan on earth will not work unless you do. You must commit to acting with determination, persistence, and patience.

If every other step was taken ... if you have the desire, the belief, if you can measure your progress, if you've written it down, seen the benefits, know where you are and what you need to do; if you've set deadlines and identified obstacles, if you've visually represented your goals and developed your plan ... if you can see yourself having achieved it ... all you need now is to apply the effort.

Commit to doing at least one thing each day that brings you closer to achieving each of your goals.

Do not get easily discouraged ... don't quit at the first sign of defeat ... don't let others stop you with their negative attitudes. Winners pick themselves up after being knocked down, and overcome all obstacles.

It may seem a bit overwhelming, but don't worry. Schedule sufficient time to work through your blueprint and take it one step at a time. Commit to getting started. Take the first step.

Creating a successful future takes energy, effort and concentrated thinking. That's the reason most people don't do it. Accept the challenge. Focus. The rewards will be worth it. Make the effort now!

"Whatever you can do, or dream you can do, begin it. Boldness has genius, power and magic in it."
Goethe

Direction Exercises

Personal Legacy Statement

Use this fantasy obituary to help you determine what matters most to you in your life. It might appear rather macabre, but it's an effective way to focus in on what is truly important to you. When doing this, write about yourself not as you are now, but as you ideally want to be. Use your imagination to create a memorial that is a fitting tribute to a lifetime of hard work and contribution.

- How do you want to be remembered?
- What professional and career goals would you hope to have achieved?
- What sort of relationships do you want to have enjoyed?
- Where would you like to be living?
- What impact would you have had over your family?
- How would you like your friends and peers to remember you?
- What legacy would you like to have left?
- What do you need to die in peace?

Prepare your fantasy obituary by completing the form below. Open your mind and let it run free. Include any and all ambitions yet to be achieved.

_____ (your name) died last night aged _____ ,

in _____ (where you would most enjoy living). He/She

worked as a _____ (desired career) achieving the position of

_____ (how high you hope to rise). He/She is

best remembered by peers for _____

_____

Personally, he/she enjoyed _____

_____

(hobbies, leisure activities, interests). His/her personal achievements included

_____

_____

and will best be remembered for _____

_____

_____

His/Her closest friends knew he/she was satisfied with her life and ready to leave this physical world because _____

_____

_____

_____

_____

_____

Priority Draw for Career Goals

Here's an exercise you can use if you're having difficulty determining the priority of your goals. List all of your career goals and ambitions on the left-hand side of this sheet. Just let your mind run free and write out up to 16 of them. This is the preliminary round. Decide which of the opposing goals you want more, and move it on to the next round. Repeat this process until you eventually have one main career goal that means the most to you.

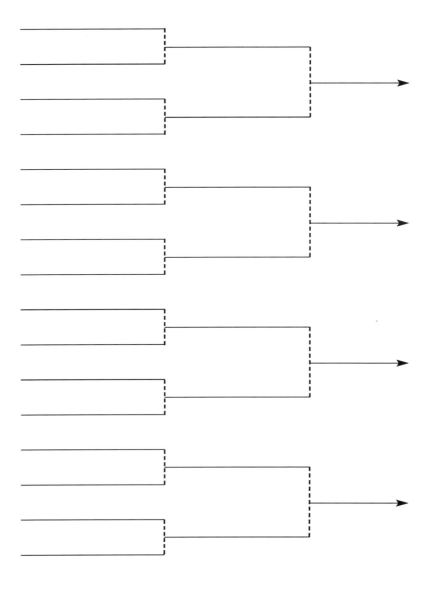

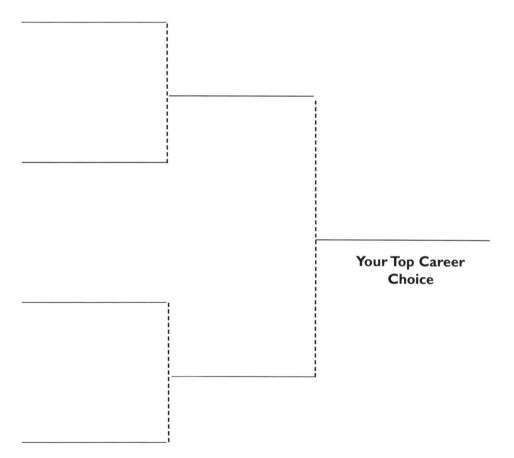

Your Top Career Choice

Priority Draw for Family/Relationship Goals

Repeat this exercise to determine the priority of your family/relationship goals. List all of your family goals and ambitions on the left-hand side of this sheet. Just let your mind run free and write up to 16 things that would bring joy to you in your family or relationships. Decide which of the opposing goals you want more, and move it on to the next round. Repeat this process until you eventually have one main family/relationship goal that means the most to you.

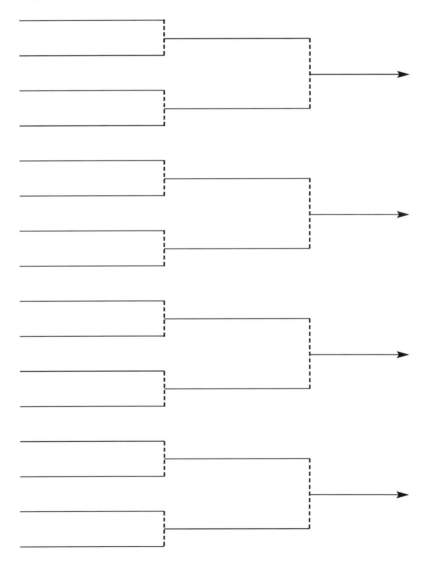

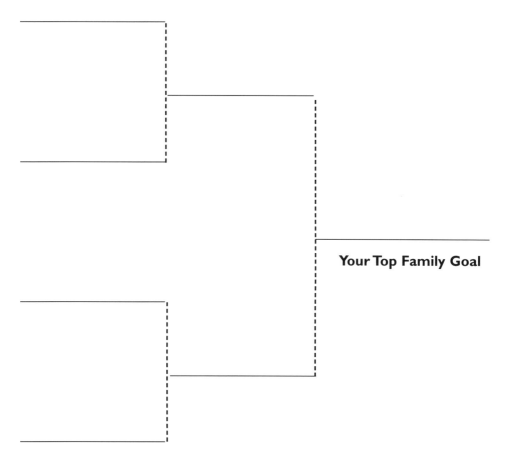

Your Top Family Goal

Priority Draw for Personal Goals

Our personal goals are the things we'd like to do for ourselves that we usually put aside then neglect as we care for our family and careers. Repeat this exercise to determine the priority of your personal goals. List everything you've always wanted to do for yourself on the left-hand side of this sheet. Let your mind run free and write up to 16 things that would bring you joy, pride, satisfaction,

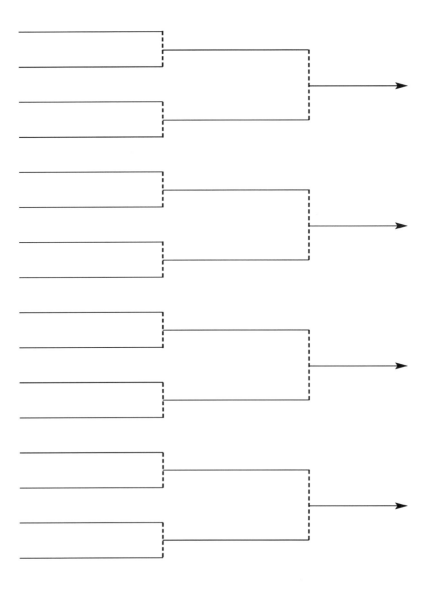

development or enlightenment. Decide which of the opposing goals you want more, and move it on to the next round. Repeat this process until you eventually have one main personal goal that would mean the most to you.

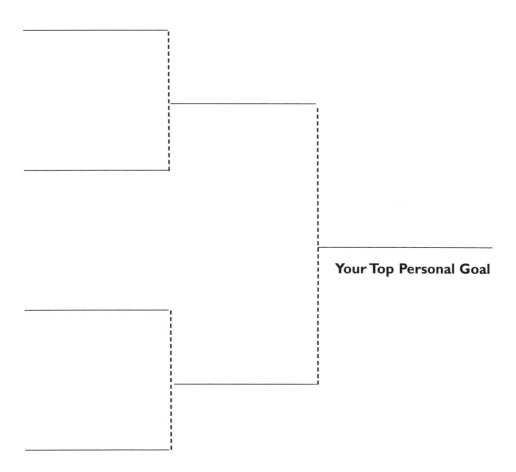

Your Top Personal Goal

Goal Achievement Worksheet

This written exercise is a valuable tool that will help you reach your most important goals. You'll visualize your goal as being real, develop a plan for accomplishing it, and develop the discipline to carry it out. Use this exercise for each of your top goals.

Begin by selecting the most important goals you identified in your priority draw sheets. Make it absolutely specific, then begin the exercise by writing it out. Refer to the goal setting checklist on pages 78 - 79 for further explanation of each of these questions. You can use this worksheet, or if you'd prefer, type out or write your answers on a separate sheet of paper that you can post and see each day.

1. Specific Goal

_____

_____

_____

_____

2. Checklist:

Do I really want it?	Yes ___	No ___
Do I believe I can do it?	Yes ___	No ___
Is it specific enough?	Yes ___	No ___
Will it be obvious to others when I reach it?	Yes ___	No ___
Is there a reasonable deadline to achieve it?	Yes ___	No ___
Is it challenging?	Yes ___	No ___
Is it meaningful?	Yes ___	No ___
Does it align with my values?	Yes ___	No ___
Is it moderately flexible?	Yes ___	No ___

If you answered 'No' to any of these questions, rewrite your goal so that it changes to a 'Yes'.

3. What will it do for me? What does it look like?

_____

_____

_____

_____

4. Current Status ... where am I now as a starting point?

_____

_____

_____

_____

5. Obstacles ... what is standing in the way? What do I have to overcome?

_____

_____

_____

_____

6. What knowledge is required ... how do I get it?

_____

_____

_____

_____

7. What people, groups, and organizations can help me?

_____

_____

_____

_____

8. The Plan ... what am I going to do, and by when?

_____

_____

_____

_____

Action Steps

Completion Deadline

1. Write out a goals card _____

2. Put together a Picture Goals Book _____

3. Share my goal with someone I respect _____

4. _____ _____

5. _____ _____

6. _____ _____

7. _____ _____

8. _____ _____

9. _____ _____

10. _____ _____

11. _____ _____

12. _____ _____

13. _____ _____

14. _____ _____

15. _____ _____

16. _____ _____

17. _____ _____

18. _____ _____

19. _____ _____

20. _____ _____

21. _____ _____

22. _____ _____

23. _____ _____

24. _____ _____

Set up Your Reward System

Some people are 'hard on themselves' or find it difficult to forgive themselves for failure or disappointments. Many people set themselves high standards which they inevitably fail to reach from time to time.

Being able to treat yourself is the necessary balance to setting yourself high standards. High standards drive us to achievement, satisfaction and a sense of accomplishment, but are only effective in the long run if balanced with the ability to pamper or reward ourselves with little treats at appropriate times.

Treats are rewards or gifts you give yourself, with a clear conscience, for hard work or hard times. They are often little things which give us great pleasure - a walk in the woods at lunchtime, an hour with a good book, a sauna or time in the whirlpool.

Stuck for ideas about treats? You can get lots of ideas by asking your friends or peers what they do, or by looking out for interesting ways to reward yourself. Here are some that might get your mind working: Having a hot bath with Epson salts; taking the afternoon off to spend in nature; doing the crossword; having lunch with someone you really like; spending uninterrupted time with your kids or spouse; buying yourself flowers; taking a nap in the middle of the day; lying in the sun watching the planes take off and land; buying a good book or magazine; going away for the weekend; playing a round of golf.

Step 1: Write down all the ways you treat yourself, or wish you could.

_____

_____

_____

_____

Step 2: Look at your month ahead and plan some treats to reward yourself after tough meetings, hard days, unpleasant tasks, major efforts etc.

Action_____ Reward _____

Action_____ Reward _____

Action_____ Reward _____

Action_____ Reward _____

Action_____ Reward _____

Things To Do
for Direction

1. Realize that if you don't decide where you are going, you'll end up where someone else wants to take you.
2. Maintain balance. Choose one thing you want for your relationships, career and yourself.
3. Do the work in the preceding exercises.
4. Remind yourself daily what you want out of life.
5. Create a collage or book with pictures of what your goals look like.
6. Burn your bridges and have faith that you can achieve anything you want to in life.
7. Do one thing each day that brings you closer to achieving your goals.
8. Close your eyes and visualize yourself already having achieved your goals.
9. Use positive affirmations every morning
10. Look for opportunities that seem to magically open up for you.

"Is it ten minutes to five already?"

chapter six

Time Management...
_____ Planning and Implementation

Action Lists

All great managers of time work from action lists every day. They discipline themselves to write things down. Every assignment, every call they have to make, every communication that's required, every appointment, every name and every phone number. They write down everything that is important.

Success isn't so much a mystery ... it's a reflection of what you are doing with your time. Highly successful people are massive action takers. They don't just try one solution to a problem, they come at it from many different directions and use action lists to record and track their efforts.

Those who do not use lists forget things ... as much as they contend not to. They cannot prioritize properly, they can't find important things to accomplish during small windows of time. They respond to the urgent instead of the important. People who rely on memory feel stressed, tired and fatigued. At the end of a day, they're unsure of what they've actually accomplished to bring them closer to their goals.

List users are more organized all day long and get the most important things done each day. They are in control of their time and their lives, on top of their work each day, move closer to their goals each day, and have a sense of accomplishment.

There's never enough time to do everything, but there's always enough time to do the important things. When action lists are written down and prioritized you can tell at-a-glance what you should do next ... you'll know right away what the most valuable use of your time is right now.

Prioritizing your action list

Martin Taylor, Vice Chairman of Hanson Trust, claims: "The greatest test of time management is making your priority choices". It can be hard to decide which of several jobs, all demanding urgent attention, should be tackled first. You're not alone ... a survey of 1300 managers showed poor priority setting was a common weakness.

The 80/20 rule applies to time management as well as it does anywhere. Diligent priority setting tells you the 20% of activities which generate 80% of your results, and has you do them before other less valuable tasks.

Priorities are determined by evaluating the importance and urgency of each item as it relates to reaching your goals and objectives. If it's both important and urgent, it's a top priority; if it is only one or the other, it's a medium priority; if it's neither, it's a low priority. With a little practice you can learn to discriminate quite quickly.

"Productivity is the deliberate, strategic investment of your time, intelligence, energy, resources and opportunities in a manner calculated to move you measurably closer to meaningful goals."
Dan Kennedy
o B.S. Time
Management

Here are some techniques you can use to help you prioritize:

If you were called out of town for a week, what is the one thing you'd do? Write a number 1 beside it. If you could do two things, what would the second thing be, put a 2 beside it. Prioritize your list numerically.

If that doesn't work for you, use a lettering system; identify the critically important things you want to achieve tomorrow morning and put an A beside them. Put B's beside the next things you want to do but are less urgent or important. Put C's beside the actions you want to do later in the day, or which could be delayed if necessary. If you're really ambitious you can then numerically order each of you're A's, B's and C's in the order you want to complete them.

It doesn't matter how long your list is, or how you decide to prioritize it, the critical part is that they have to be prioritized. This allows you to concentrate on what you're doing while you're doing it, knowing that it's the most important thing you could be doing with your time right now. You won't be overwhelmed by everything you want or need to do each day. Instead, you can be completely present to what you're doing while your doing it. This is truly where joy and fulfillment exists.

Daily Planning and Organizing

"The art of living successfully consists of being able to hold two opposite ideas in tension at the same time; first, to make long term plans as if we were going to live forever; and, second, to conduct ourselves daily as if we are going to die tomorrow."

Sydney Harris

Alec Mackenzie, author of the best seller, 'The Time Trap', claims that planning goals and priority tasks for the day is the most important activity in time management. And to make sure the planning sticks, you must write it all down.

A written daily plan is essential

Nothing that you do in your attempts to manage your time will be more valuable than your written plan. A daily plan will guarantee that you get your top priority tasks done; guide you in determining the priorities of new tasks that arise during the day; give you psychological backup for resisting interruptions; and tell you what to return to when you do get interrupted.

Your written plan puts you in control of your time. Effective time management strategies utilize monthly, weekly and daily planning. There are advantages to each of them, but your daily actions are driven by your daily plan.

Use the right tool for the job

Exactly how you choose to write up your plan, in which format or in which kind of physical planning system are less important than the fact that you do it. The key however, is that your daily planning system is a tool that must be as integrated as possible. Combining calendar, diary, to-do list, phone directory, and an area for notes will eliminate all those scraps of paper and sticky notes that hinder your effectiveness. The more portable it is, the better, so that you can take it everywhere. Those readers who utilize technology to it's maximum will be tempted to consider using their PDA's as their time management tool. Do yourself a favour and forget it. Programming and retrievability is still more time consuming than if you use a manual planning system. Use your PDA for alarms and database management, not for planning each day.

"Finish each day and be done with it. You have done what you could; some blunders and absurdities no doubt crept in - forget them as soon as you can. Tomorrow is a new day; you shall begin it well and serenely."
Ralph Waldo Emerson

99

Here's a checklist for your time management tool

It must be functional

It must have a place for everything you have to do or remember, it must be instantly available for quick recording, and it must include a pen or pencil.

It must provide ease of retrievability

Items must be recorded and placed were they can be easily retrieved, at-a-glance, even if they were recorded months ago.

It must be integrated

Replace the many separate pieces of paper that used to clutter up your desk and your mind ... calendar, action lists, phone messages, sticky notes etc.

It must quick and easy to use

You must be able to use it and refer to its contents immediately.

It must keep your goals visible

Write out your family, business and development goals so that you can see them all day. Write down the three most important, most significant, most productive, most valuable things you can do to foster success, and translate them into specific actions.

"Happiness is not a destination, it is a process or a condition. A person is only happy when they are engaged in activities that give them a sense of personal growth, achievement and contribution."
Aristotle

It must have enough room for notes

An ideal dayplanner is two pages per day, giving you designated areas for your appointments, phone calls, action lists, and daily notes of importance.

How To Plan Your Day

Each evening open up tomorrow's pages. The timing seems to be best just as you are wrapping up the day and things are still fresh in your mind. You'll see any early morning appointments in time to reset your alarm if that's required.

1. Write out your goals and objectives for tomorrow, keeping them top of mind

2. Start your action list by writing the things you did not accomplish from today's list.

3. List three things you will do to bring you closer to each of your goals.

4. List the things that you will do to generate value for your employer.

5. List anything else of importance that you'd like to do tomorrow.

6. Write out everyone you have to call, and include their phone number so you don't have to look it up each time you try to reach them.

7. Write down everyone you have to talk to ... make notes to remind you of the different things you have to discuss with each person, a mini agenda for every contact.

8. Write numbers or letters beside each action that indicates the order in which you will achieve them.

9. Close the book on your day and relax! Leave your work on those pages, not cluttering up your mind.

How to Use Your Dayplanner

It should become a part of your anatomy ... you should feel lost without it. (In fact, this is a good time to insist that you write your name and phone number on the front page in case you do lose it.) For maximum effectiveness, combine it with your telephone book, chequebook, business card holder or whatever else fits your style or needs. The secret to successfully implementing your plan is simply to follow it. Work diligently from your plan all day long. Carry it with you wherever you go, completing your tasks one at a time, starting with your top priority.

First Things First

The key to successful time management is doing the most important thing first, and giving it your full concentration, to the exclusion of everything else. Do the first thing first - not after checking the mail, not after reading the paper, not after a couple of small jobs ...DO IT FIRST

Start with number one on your list and do it.

Work single-mindedly on that one item until its conclusion. Banish all thought of the rest of your list from your conscious mind. Be completely present to what you are doing right at this very moment. Relish it, enjoy it. Don't think of anything else you have to do. Be proud of the fact that right now you are doing the most important thing you can.

Work from your dayplanner all day long

When you finish number 1 on your action list, move on to number 2, and so forth, working your way through as many items as you can each day. As you accomplish each task in its order, cross it off your list. If you can't complete it because of something outside of your control, circle its priority number and come

One Day From The Author's Dayplanner

Appointments

Prioritized action list for today

Phone calls I plan to make today

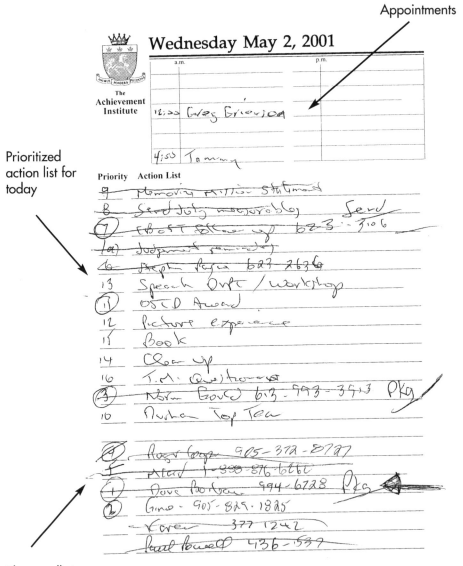

This is what I want to
remember and take
action on every day

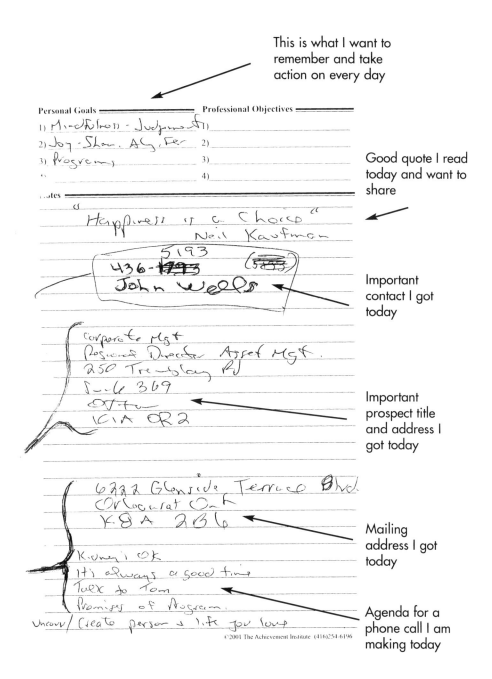

Good quote I read
today and want to
share

Important
contact I got
today

Important
prospect title
and address I
got today

Mailing
address I got
today

Agenda for a
phone call I am
making today

©2001 The Achievement Institute (416)254-6196

back to it later.

As you set up appointments, write them into the appropriate day immediately. If you plan to follow up with someone on a particular day then go to that page in your dayplanner, write in their name and phone number and any helpful notes that will jog your memory. If one of your phone calls couldn't be completed today, write it down on tomorrow's page.

As more tasks present themselves, evaluate them immediately against the next item on your list. If it's more important, do it now. If it's not, add it to the bottom of your existing list and determine and record priorities, i.e: if it's more important than #6, but less important than #7, you can make it 6(a). Anything else of importance for you to remember, or that you need for future reference, write it down on your note-taking page.

Concentrate on what you're doing while you're doing it

The trick to being productive when you have many, sometimes conflicting, responsibilities, is to be able to focus on the one thing you are dealing with right now. Be 100% in the moment. If you let your mind wander to anything but the one thing you are working on right now, productivity evaporates. Concentration is everything. Highly productive people in all fields are able to achieve this kind of total concentration. Anyone can do it, all it takes is practice and effort.

If you make this one change you will see profound improvements in the use and enjoyment of your time, including these immediate benefits. You'll be doing your most important task when you're at your best, and be more successful doing it. It's much easier to resist interruptions, as few things will seem as important as your top priority. Even if nothing else gets done because of unexpected problems, you know you've completed your top priority.

"I never could have done without the habits of punctuality, order and diligence... the determination to concentrate myself on one subject at a time."

Charles Dickens

Work Uninterrupted

If you're working on a task that requires absolute mental focus you must work completely uninterrupted. This means closing your door if you have an office, getting the switchboard to take messages, turning on your voice mail, moving to a boardroom, or putting up a do-not-disturb sign. You'll get more done.

Have Integrity in the Moment of Decision

Each day we are faced with moments of decision. It is these moments that define the difference between success and mediocrity. Moments immediately following the accomplishment of a task, moments after phone calls, after meetings, as soon as we arrive in the morning, when we get an idea or see an opportunity; when the alarm rings, when our peers go out for a smoke break.

All greatness comes with having integrity in the moment of decision. Integrity to do what it is you should do, not what you want to do. Integrity in facing temptation, and resisting it. Make your decisions, in each moment, based on what it is you truly want out of life.

Maximizing Your Time

Use your dayplanner to empower you seven days a week

Remember, it is not important that you use a specific dayplanner, or that you organize it in specific ways. What is important is that you organize it so that it is most comfortable and appropriate for you, and empowers you to make the most effective use of your time every day. If you're going shopping, or doing errands, or running the kids around on the weekend, use it to keep track of what you want to do or buy. Use it to make your life easier, easing your stress and allowing you to be the most effective you can be in achieving what you want in your life.

Minimize unplanned activity

Most people just show up at the office, work and react. All of their unscheduled time gets used up. By reducing unscheduled and unplanned activity, you automatically reduce waste.

Profit from open time

Utilize waiting time, commuting time, unexpected spare moments. Turn your car into a classroom, using audio tapes to increase your knowledge, motivation and productivity. Always be prepared to flesh out ideas, plan a project, or prepare for an upcoming meeting. Make your calls from a cell phone while you're out of the office. Keep a reading file in your briefcase that you can refer to when you have a few found moments.

"There is nothing so precious as to be in the moment.... our hearts sing, our minds flourish and our spirits soar"
Barbara De Angelis

Live off-peak

Do things when others aren't ... avoid the bank Friday afternoons, don't leave yourself a rush-hour drive back to the office, avoid line-ups during the noon hour period when most people have their time off.

Do your nuisance chores

Nothing is so fatiguing as the eternal nagging of an incomplete task. From time to time a necessary 'chore' that is distasteful will keep getting delayed - an accounting matter, a report, whatever. Don't keep moving it to the bottom of the pile. The best thing to do with such a nuisance is to do it and get rid of it as quickly as possible. It isn't like wine ... it won't improve with age. The longer you let it hang around, the more of a distraction it will become, and the less you'll want to do it.

Drop time-robbing tasks
Again, if the 80/20 rule applies to your day, eight out of 10 tasks which you currently do are bandits intent on stealing your time. Some obvious inessential tasks include reading junk mail or any non-work related reading, socializing on the telephone, walking to someone's desk instead of using the phone, etc. Drop these like a lead balloon and you'll gain valuable time.

Eliminate perfectionism
It's a death trap that causes you to either delay important activities, or spend too long on them. Never carry on beyond the point where the task is sufficiently well done to achieve your purpose. Help yourself eliminate unnecessary perfectionism by deadlining your tasks, by asking yourself 'how good is good enough', or by breaking large tasks down into manageable pieces. If perfectionism presents problems for you, you'll find more ways to deal with it later in the book.

Batching tasks
Whenever possible, batch work together, so that you make all your phone calls one after another, or deal with all your mail in one session. Dodging between very different tasks is ineffective since it takes time for your brain to make adjustments. Batching tasks takes advantage of the learning curve. The more similar tasks you complete in one timeframe, the more efficient you become.

"Success seems to be connected with action. Successful people keep moving. They make mistakes, but they don't quit."
Conrad Hilton

Time Blocking
A real hidden secret of peak performers is that they schedule unbreakable appointments with themselves that they religiously keep: writing projects, developing ideas, completing projects, doing research, etc. This commits them to spending time on projects that otherwise get put aside for more pressing matters. If someone wants to see you during your scheduled private time, simply tell them you have a previous appointment, then lock yourself away from interruptions by closing your door, going into a boardroom, library or working from home.

Avoid Procrastination
Procrastination is a thief of time. Avoid procrastination by developing a sense of urgency. The person who immediately moves into action often outperforms those with intelligence, education and experience, and continues to hold the leading edge throughout their career.

Develop a Sense of Urgency

Most people work slowly ... just watch them. Work expands to fill their time. It is extremely difficult to instill a continuing, constant sense of urgency when one does not naturally exist, but if it really matters to you that a letter gets to the mailbox for the 4:00 pm pickup, then you will automatically accomplish more than just about anyone else, because those things don't matter to them. Learn to DO IT NOW - you'll get more done.

Moments of decision should also be faced with a sense of urgency. DO IT NOW. Less than 2% of the population has a sense of urgency, and this 2% are, without exception, among the most successful, accomplished group of people in the world. Jump on an opportunity now, because it may not exist later. Call that lead now, because they may leave the country tomorrow. When you have something to do, rise above your peers and accomplish more by DOING IT NOW!

Effective Delegation

Delegation is the key activity of every successful manager. Its direct and indirect benefits are significant, if not powerful.

In 'The Power of Focus', Jack Canfield and his co-authors encourage readers to focus on their natural talents. Do the things you are brilliant at and delegate everything else. When you focus most of your time and energy doing the things you are truly brilliant at, you eventually reap big rewards. This may not be practical in all cases, but there is truth in the message.

Relinquish Your Need to Control

Effective delegation begins with developing the ability to relinquish control. You will never master delegation unless you can let go and place trust in others. Give up your need to know everything. Give up the artificial value you place in having your finger on the pulse of your whole organization. Your value is not determined by what you know, it's determined by what your team accomplishes. Maximum effectiveness can be accomplished only by empowering your team members to exercise both the authority needed for tasks and the responsibility for the means to achieve them.

Your Personal Assistant

The most crucial individual in terms of increasing your productivity through delegation is your personal assistant, for those fortunate enough to have one.

> *"A single idea can revolutionize your life, but ideas are like slippery fish; you've got to write them down so they don't get away."*
> Earl Nightingale

We're not referring to a receptionist, secretary or someone else whose duties you share with two or three other people. A true personal assistant is someone who is dedicated to you, and is extraordinary at doing the things you don't like or shouldn't be doing. The main role of this person is to free you up from all of the mundane tasks and responsibilities that clutter up your week. Their role is to protect you so that you can focus on achieving those key things which impact your success.

Daily Delegation

In your daily work situation you should delegate as much and as often as possible, but restrict delegation to your direct subordinates. Don't delegate only to the most capable, or to those with the most free time, but consider staff members who want to take on more difficult tasks, who need experience, and whose abilities need to be tested and developed.

Benefits of Delegation

1. Delegation makes things easier for managers and helps them gain valuable time for important responsibilities such as true leadership.

"All the treasures of earth cannot bring back one lost moment."
French Proverb

2. Delegation capitalizes on the knowledge and experience of subordinates.
3. Delegation helps to further and develop the abilities, initiative, independence and competencies of subordinates.
4. Delegation has a positive effect on the motivation and job satisfaction of subordinates.

Methods of Delegation

Task Delegation is the most immediate. Specific tasks or subtasks are assigned with little or no responsibility for the bigger picture. This is base delegation, is the easiest to relinquish, yet is the least rewarding for your team members.

Function Delegation involves a group of tasks related to one particular activity such as sales, research or accounting. This needn't involve major responsibilities, but requires initiative for developing multiple task systems and brings satisfaction.

Goal Delegation refers to the achievement of an end result and the various tasks necessary to fulfill this objective: increase sales by 10 percent or successfully launch a new product. This is the most senior of delegations, empowering others to show leadership and creativity, and provides ideal opportunities for growth and evaluation of subordinates.

*"Everything
comes to him
who waits except
the time he lost
waiting."*
Public Witticism

Planning and Implementation Exercises

Priority Setting Exercise

You have to realize that you simply can't and needn't do everything ... and since you can't do it all, you need to understand how to determine the relative priority of competing tasks. This principle, attributed to General Dwight D. Eisenhower, will give you a technique to quickly decide which tasks should have priority based on their urgency and importance.

Step 1: Before committing to action, always put your task on trial by asking the following questions
a) Why am I doing this?
b) How will this help me achieve my goals or objectives?
c) Could I save time by doing it a different way?
d) Can or should this be delegated?
e) Can it be dropped entirely?

Step 2: If the task must be done, and by you, rate its importance on a scale of 1-3
1. Unimportant...would not result in major problems if not done
2. Important..........would cause serious problems if not done
3. Essential..........Must be finished

Step 3: Rate the urgency of the task using a similar scale
1. Low ....can be done at any time
2. Medium ......Must be finished this week
3. High ....Must be done today

To calculate the priority of the task, multiply the two ratings. For example, a task which is essential with a high urgency receives a rating of 3 x 3 = 9. However, another essential task which has a low urgency factor, would only be rated 3 x 1 = 3.

Practical Exercise

Take a half dozen of your tasks that are pending and calculate the priority of each using the Eisenhower principle:

Task   Importance x   Urgency =   Priority

_____   _____ x _____ = _____

_____   _____ x _____ = _____

_____   _____ x _____ = _____

_____   _____ x _____ = _____

_____   _____ x _____ = _____

_____   _____ x _____ = _____

_____   _____ x _____ = _____

_____   _____ x _____ = _____

Asking Exercise

There is power in learning to ask for things in life. Quite often all that we want is right there for the asking, we're just not comfortable enough to ask for it. If you sell for a living, if you can increase your comfort level with asking, and your productivity, by completing the following exercise.

1. Today, ask somebody for something that you think is completely unreasonable. Who will you ask, and what will you ask them?

_____

2. Ask for written testimonial letters from at least three people. Who are they and when are you going to ask them?

_____

3. Ask for assistance from someone who can help you reach your goals. Who will you ask, what will you ask them and when will you do it?

_____

4. Ask two of your customers to personally introduce you to someone who would be interested in buying your product or service. Who will you ask and when will you do it?

_____

5. Ask one of your customers how you might provide better service. Who will you ask and when?

6. Ask one of the internal managers that you deal with for feedback on how you could improve the way you work with them. Who will you ask and when?

How Well Do You Delegate?

The most effective managers around the world delegate as much and as often as possible. Complete this self-test by answering Yes or No to determine if you are delegating well.

1. Do I work long office hours? Do I take work home on a regular basis? . . . .   Yes   No

2. Do I consistently work longer than my staff? . . . .   Yes   No

3. Do I spend time on things for other people that they could do themselves? . . . .   Yes   No

4. In an emergency, would there be trouble finding a subordinate or colleague who would relieve me? . . . .   Yes   No

5. Do I lack the time to plan my tasks and activities? .   Yes   No

6. When I return from a business trip is my desk piled high? . . . .   Yes   No

7. Do I still deal with activities and problems that were my responsibility before I got promoted? . . . .   Yes   No

8. Do I often have to postpone an important task to deal with others? . . . .   Yes   No

9. Do I spend time on routine work that could be done by someone else? . . . .   Yes   No

10. Am I constantly checking to see if the details are being adequately dealt with? . . . .   Yes   No

11. Do I lack the time for social or company functions? .... Yes   No

12. Do I want to be involved in and informed about everything? .... Yes   No

13. Do I lack a personal assistant who can accept appropriate delegation? .... Yes   No

Add how many times you answered Yes.

0-3   You delegate extraordinarily well and don't need any further direction.

4-7   You could improve your delegation style in several areas.

8 +   You have a serious problem with delegation. Solving this problem should be an absolute priority for you.

Things To Do
For Effective Planning and Implementation

1. Use a daily integrated dayplanning system similar to the sample shown on pages 102 & 103.
2. Write a prioritized action list for every day.
3. Do first things first, to completion.
4. Don't be perfect if perfect isn't required
5. Give high priority to important things you find distasteful.
6. Develop a sense of urgency.
7. Maximize your time.
8. Shut yourself off when working on activities that require concentration.
9. Concentrate on what you are doing, while you're doing it.
10 Schedule time in your calendar to work on strategic planning, long term projects or activities that require long periods of concentration.
11. Delegate effectively and delegate often.

"What are you crying for? I promise
you'll have it back by tomorrow"

chapter seven

Time Management...
Personal Habits

How to Establish New Habits

"Far better it is to dare mighty things, to win glorious triumphs, even though checkered by failure, than to rank with those poor spirits who neither enjoy much nor suffer much, because they live in the grey twilight that knows no victory or defeat."

Theodore Roosevelt

Planning new ways to do things is relatively easy; sticking with them is the really tough part. To reinforce new behaviour, use the following ideas suggested by 19th century American psychologist, William James, which were added to by the Carlson Learning Company.

Identify the Habit you Want to Change
You must pinpoint the precise behaviours you want to change. Use the exercises in this book to uncover actions and behaviours that limit your performance. The more you know about what you do, and when you do it, the easier it will be to identify habits that are holding you back.

Precisely Define your New Habit

Use the goals and objectives exercise in this book to identify what you want to work towards and how you plan to do it. Describe the new habit or behaviour and the frequency with which it must be exhibited. Develop a realistic action plan and get started.

Commit to specific actions

You can't make changes unless you commit to taking specific action. Saying you want to manage your time better just doesn't cut it. You must define specific actions and habits and just do it.

Think Big

Give your new habits every chance of success by launching them strongly. Create whatever reminders and visual prompts you wish. Announce your plans to as many people as you appropriately can. Work out a buddy arrangement; find a coach. In short, surround your resolution with every possible aid ... this gives you momentum against the temptation to backslide.

Start right away and practice often

Seize the first possible chance to act out your new methods, and take advantage of every opportunity. It's repetition that ingrains new behaviour - thinking about it will not.

"If no one ever took risks, Michelangelo would have painted on the Sistine floor."
Neil Simon

Don't make exceptions

A lapse is like skidding when you're driving your car. It takes much more effort to recover control than to maintain it from the start. A slip can diminish the energy of all further attempts. Exceptions cause the foundation to crumble.

Set up a System of Reinforcement

Build a strong support team that will encourage and reward you for staying with it. Consider those you most trust, who are in a position to see the new behaviour. Share your commitment with them and have them commit to watching you. Use the behavioural contract at the end of this book to set up personal rewards for maintaining action on your commitments.

Eliminate Your Procrastination

"Hold yourself responsible for a higher standard than anybody else expects of you. Never excuse yourself. Never pity yourself. Be a hard taskmaster to yourself, be lenient with everybody else."

Henry Ward Beecher

There's a Spanish proverb that says we should start each day by eating a live frog! Whenever possible do the thing you least want to do first. If you postpone disagreeable tasks until later in the day, chances are it will subconsciously effect you all day, distracting you from enjoying what you are doing while you are doing it.

Realize that you are in control

The first, and most critical step in overcoming procrastination is to realize that you are in control, then make the commitment to change. Recognize that for whatever reason, you have developed the habit of putting things off, and remind yourself that you are capable of replacing that bad habit with a better one if you choose to. Procrastination is within you; it's something you do to yourself. You can change it, and you will if you have enough determination. Make a conscious effort to develop a do-it-now attitude. Develop a sense of urgency!

Be honest with yourself

If you're putting something off, don't pretend otherwise. Ask yourself the relative importance of these things, and why you don't like doing them. Are they the same kinds of things you delay every time? Are they critical to your success or failure, are they unnatural, do they conflict with your values? If they are critical to the job you are doing, yet you find them completely distasteful you need to question whether you belong in that job at all.

"The world is full of willing people, some willing to work, the rest willing to let them."
Robert Frost

There are several key forms of procrastination. Identify which one you suffer from and take the necessary action to overcome it.

Perfectionism Procrastination

The story is told of the university professor who constantly boasted how one day he would write the definitive book about his field of study, Flemish politics. Finally tiring of this, his students locked him in his office and said they would release him only when the first page of his masterpiece was completed. Many hours later, surrounded by hundreds of sheets of discarded paper, the academic collapsed in tears over his typewriter. He had been unable to finish a single sentence, let alone a complete page to his satisfaction. Every word he wrote

119

struck him as falling so short of perfection he began all over again.

By continuously striving for perfection, you create delays. While it is admirable to do everything to the best of your abilities, in the real world, perfect isn't as always as good as adequate if adequate is all that is required to achieve the objective. Constantly ask yourself what each situation or task really requires.

Boredom Procrastination

There are certain tasks, which although essential, are less interesting than watching paint dry. Human nature draws us towards those activities we find most rewarding and away from chores which are tedious. The consequence of being bored is often procrastination. Deal with this by forcing yourself to give high priority to those tasks which you find uninteresting.

Hostility Procrastination

We are sometimes filled with negative emotions toward individuals who assign our work, towards the company, or towards the work itself. Resentment often causes delay in accomplishing certain tasks. Use the power of your mind to control these negative emotions, and give those tasks a high priority. Delaying them blocks your flow.

Eliminate Procrastination in Others

"Don't wait for your ship to come in; swim out to it."
Anonymous

If people on your team have trouble with procrastination, you can help in several ways. Neil Fiore, in 'The Now Habit' identifies four steps that will help you deal with procrastinators.

Build confidence by fostering commitment, not compliance

Allowing others to participate in decisions which affect them increases their commitment. Instead of saying, "You have to have it in by noon", change it to "Considering what you know about our schedule, when do you think you could have this part done?"

Focus on starting rather than finishing things

The idea of being held accountable for a major project with a lengthy deadline makes procrastinators anxious; they feel overwhelmed by the immensity of the task. Reduce the fear by focusing on the starting point. Instead of saying, "Remember, the deadline is only two months away," say "When can you get started on a rough outline?"

Give criticism constructively.

Angry, negative criticism is always destructive, and even more so with those who procrastinate. Fearing for their survival, they lose whatever ability they had to focus on priorities. Don't say, "This report totally misses the point." Instead say, "This is a good start. If we can add a couple of thoughts on A and B and strengthen the conclusion, we'll have a winner." Let team members know you recognize their worth as people, and reward progress along the way.

Be decisive and set priorities.

Managers who tend to shift priorities as new problems arise are legendary. This is also very damaging to team members and their productivity. Some will be tempted to say, "Let's just wait a day or so and see if they change their minds again". Shift priorities only for confirmed emergencies. Change assignments only if other priorities are also considered, and alternate the team members you choose for each crisis situation.

Powerful Listening

Some of the biggest foul-ups, the things that really waste our time, are the result of poor listening. Poor listening skills are one of the most consistent, most common weaknesses acknowledged by professionals in every field. Here are some of the best techniques for developing a powerful listening personality.

Listen as if there will be a test afterwards.

Pay attention. Most ineffective listening is the result of assumptions that the speaker or their message is unimportant. Listen as if the speaker is the most important person in the world, and that your memory of their message determines whether you pass or fail in life.

> *"When I listen I have power, when I speak I give it away."*
> Voltaire

Develop the desire to learn through listening

If you're motivated to listen it's more likely that you will.

Don't be competitive in the communication process

It's not a contest or a debate to see who can convince the other side that they are right or better. Control your ego, not the conversation.

Calmly question. Don't harshly interrogate

Your attitude, your tone of voice, your demeanor will determine the quality of the communication.

Concentrate completely. Drop everything

Our rate of listening is 5 times faster than the average speaking rate, so it takes a concentrated effort to pay attention. Drop everything and give the speaker your full undivided attention. Concentrate completely on what the other person is saying. Don't let your mind wander, don't interrupt, don't think about what you will say in response. Don't answer the phone, don't look at your watch, don't shuffle paper, don't write unless you have to take notes, don't answer the phone ... in other words, don't do anything else except listen.

Positively reinforce the speaker

Good listening takes work. Part of the job is to let the speaker know you are listening. Acknowledge what they've said by nodding, repeat key points, encourage the speaker to continue, then paraphrase.

Learn from what the speaker is saying

Don't just listen for facts, listen for what the facts are being used to convey. Ask yourself how you can use this information, what value does it have. Don't listen as if you're waiting for your turn to speak, or even think about your response. Do not interrupt the speaker.

Keep an open mind

"A good listener is not only popular everywhere but after a while he knows something."
Wilson Mizner

Be calm and peaceful, and stop listening defensively. Ignore any prejudices, don't make assumptions, don't overreact to emotionally charged words or comments. Perhaps you don't like being called 'dear', or you find the loud laugh irritating. Ignore these mannerisms and stay focused on what is being said, rather than how it is said.

Be an active listener

Detect and interpret gestures, expressions, tone of voice and clarify their meaning. Ask relevant questions to clarify the message. Take notes, but just the key words to help reinforce your understanding.

Listen with your whole body

Maintain eye contact, but don't stare unnaturally. Lean into the speaker, uncross your arms and legs, don't fidget.

Acknowledge and deal with feelings

If the speaker's emotions appear to be influencing the communication. simply verify them in a non-judgmental way. "You seem pretty upset about this?" By asking, you acknowledge that their feelings are important to you. You also avoid having to deal with feelings that you only perceive, and that might not even be related to the current communication.

Use silence appropriately
A pause that allows for reflection shows respect and allows your communication partner to give a response that is accurate, not hurried.

Clarify what is relevant then move on
Once you have the importance of the speaker's message and all the relevant information, politely excuse yourself and move on with the rest of your day.

Positive Delay and Saying No

"Delay is preferable to error."
Thomas Jefferson

There are always more things to do than available time ... more calls to make, more people to talk to, more places to go, more details to check up on. This problem doesn't diminish with success; it increases. For the person who aspires to excellence it is emotionally difficult to leave things undone, to know there are things that should have been done that weren't.

"If you want a quick answer, it's No."
Buyer's slogan

Make the effort to adjust your thinking
You can only do what you can do, nothing more. When you make your action list it's important not to hopelessly overload it. If you consistently pile on more than can be done, it becomes de-motivating, decreases productivity and reduces the opportunity to enjoy each day. Deciding what not to do is just as important as deciding what to do.

When to say No
Although a sense of urgency is critical to effective time management, there are times where there is power in positive delay. In the right circumstances, delay is preferable to wasting time.

Moving too slowly can result in missed opportunities, but on occasion moving too fast can result in costly and time consuming blunders. In addition, taking on too much can have a detrimental effect on our performance and mental strength. Eliminate demands on your time that do not bring you closer to your goals.

Delay, or refusal, is positive when:
- a low priority task is delayed in favour of a higher priority
- you are too upset, angry, fearful, or depressed to think and act clearly
- you lack information or skills to do it effectively
- you are mentally or physically exhausted
- it need not be done by you at all
- it does not bring you closer to your goals
- the request is unreasonable.

The No process
- Listen carefully to ensure you fully understand what is being asked of you
- Say No firmly, but politely. Don't build false hope with a wishy-washy answer.
- Give reasons, if appropriate. This reinforces credibility
- Offer alternatives, which demonstrates your good faith.

Exactly how to say No
- "I'm sorry, but my other commitments just won't permit me to take on another project right now".
- "I promised my family I wouldn't take on anything else this year. I've been neglecting them too much".
- "Thanks for the compliment, but I'm afraid I'll have to decline. Maybe next year".

"Diplomacy is the art of saying 'Nice doggie' until you can find a rock."
Will Rogers

Try these ideas to stop taking on too much
- Stop telling yourself you work best under pressure; nothing works best under pressure, except land mines and pressure cookers.
- Resist the urge to step in and take over because others are not doing their job; their work is their responsibility, not yours.
- Don't assume everything has to be done; learn to discriminate low priority work, and say No.
- Ask yourself if part of the problem is lack of personal organizational skills
- Stop trying to make everything perfect; some things aren't worth the extra effort.

Saying No to the boss

Almost every boss would prefer to have fewer things done well, especially if they are top priorities. Many people get overloaded because they valiantly try to do everything the boss assigns. Ask your boss to help decide the priorities in order to avoid being overloaded.

Open up your planning system, go over your top priorities with him/her, and ask where this new assignment might fit in. Do this in a positive fashion, not with resentment because you think you're being overworked!

When your boss gives you a new task, project or assignment that does not bring you closer to achieving your goals, try this: "Sure, but can I ask you a question first?" "I'm not sure if you're aware of it, but I have these priorities I'm working on right now." "I know it's not possible to do everything, and I'm not sure which to do first."

Empowering people to say No if you're the boss

Encourage your team members to point out conflicts and offer alternatives. Let them know you expect clear thinking, not blind acceptance. And if others in the organization make demands on your people, support them as they say No to unreasonable requests.

Effective Work Space

The successful and effective implementation of innovative ideas seems to come about in an organized, disciplined way. A pristine work area might be a sign of obsession that hinders effectiveness, but is preferable to the person immersed in clutter and chaos that wastes time hunting and searching, or even worse is unable to concentrate on what he is doing while he is doing it. It has been proven time and again that a cluttered work area clutters the mind and distracts from the task at hand.

It's best that you be semi-organized ... find the balance. Be honest with yourself. Is the level of clutter and disorganization around you a help, or hindrance ... is it out of control or just right? Can you find anything you want within 10 seconds?

"He and I had an office so tiny that an inch smaller and it would have been called adultery."
Dorothy Parker

Create a cockpit workspace

Picture what an airplane cockpit looks like; there are no manuals on the dash, no stack of pens, no memos, no tissues, no useless paper. It's an immensely efficient work area where the operator can reach what's required within moments.

Come as close as you can to creating your own work-space cockpit. The top of your desk, your work area, should be completely clear of all distractions, including current files you might be working on. Store items you need on a regular basis within an imaginary circle.

At the beginning of each day, review your daily plan, and retrieve the files that you require for today's projects. Keep today's work in vertical file holders on your filing cabinet. Everything else should have a home in a drawer.

125

Control your In-box

Have an in-box that is clearly marked as such, and everything that comes to your office goes into it. Make it clear to everyone that stuff doesn't go on your desk, or on your chair, or on the floor ... it goes into the In Box.

Keep your eye out for anything urgent that you're expecting, but otherwise, go through all of it at once, preferably just before lunch. Clear it each day so it doesn't pile up and become a distraction.

Control Incoming Paper

Deal with documents, inquiries, letters and memos immediately as you read them. Touch paper only once; you must either trash, file, delegate, or take action ... nothing else! Don't move it from pile to pile, don't put it aside until later, put it where it belongs right now.

If it requires action, determine the relative priority of that action. If it's top priority, do it now. If it's not, add the action to your list for proper prioritization, then trash or file the piece of paper.

If it's obvious junk mail, don't even open it ... just toss it. To save time, keep your recycling box right under your hands when opening correspondence.

Act on it if it's urgent, or write it down to take action on when it becomes a higher priority. File it if you are absolutely, positively sure you will need it again.

Filing

Many of us are in the habit of keeping papers automatically, without a clear purpose. File sparingly, and purge your files frequently. Studies have shown that as much as 60% of filed material is never looked at again ... all that excess paper gets in the way and wastes your time when you're looking for something you need. If it's just a reference document and someone else has a copy - trash it.

"It's not enough to be busy; so are the ants. The question is; What are we busy about?"
Henry David Thoreau

Open files for every client and every project. Keep different categories in different drawers if it's more effective for you, but all files, without exception, must be alphabetically stored for quick and easy retrieval.

When removing files from a drawer, mark their position so they can be returned quickly and easily to their correct place. Or even better, just remove what you need and position the file so that it sticks out from the rest.

More tips for office effectiveness
- Visible clocks that keep you aware of time.
- A comfortable chair with lumbar support.
- Hanging file folders.
- Lots of hidden storage space.

Things to avoid
- Candy jars, etc., that invite people into your work space
- Facing the door or oncoming traffic
- Positioned next to the water cooler or washroom

Pruning Mail and Office Clutter

It's been said that William Randolph Hearst never answered his mail; he claimed that after two weeks, people either came to see him, called on the phone or wrote a second letter. There's also a chief executive of a Fortune 500 company who uses what he calls a 'ninety day drawer'. All his mail goes into that drawer to 'ripen'. He says it is surprising how little of it has any importance after ninety days.

We don't necessarily recommend either technique, but there are definite ways we could be handling our mail more efficiently than we do now. By far and away the most effective way to reduce your load is to have your mail screened. Have your in-basket located on your assistants desk.

Screen your mail using this four step process.

1. Handle
As much as possible, encourage your assistant to answer routine mail. Give him/her the authority to discard when appropriate.

2. Delegate
If mail coming to you can be answered more appropriately by someone else in your department, your assistant should route it to that person. If it is critical that you know about the situation, it should be summarized it for you.

"Whatever the mind can conceive and believe, it can achieve."
Napoleon Hill

3. File
If the matter is not urgent but is something you would eventually want to read, your assistant should place the material in a review file.

4. Expedite
This leaves only those papers that require your personal attention. Work out a routine with your assistant: Have him/her scan all reading material, highlighting or flagging only information which would be of interest or importance, and leaving it in your In basket.

Clutter piles up

Magazines, letters, brochures, calendars, files, reading, piles up and up. You get buried under it all. Perhaps sometime soon you'll clean it up, but instead you just put it aside for later. If that 'over here for now' pile gets cleared regularly it can work ... but if the stuff at the bottom is three weeks old then it's not working for you.

Be ruthless around paper

If you don't need it, or won't use it again, toss it. Toss paper that you haven't looked at in the last year. When in doubt, toss it instead of keeping it. Don't be a packrat. Anything that does not assist you in some way is clutter, and impacts your effectiveness.

Try pruning your office stuff using this checklist from Mark Ellwood's, 'A Complete Waste of Time'

- Does this item contribute to the positive image that I want to convey? Throw out meaningless photographs, tacky souvenirs and dead plants.
- Is this something I need in order to operate my business? Throw out old bulletins, or file them in binders.
- Am I finished with this magazine? Quickly scan the table of contents to see if there's anything you need to keep. If something is of value, cut it out and file it.
- Is this part of my current business mission? Throw out or remove items from previous business enterprises or projects that are no longer relevant.
- Do I use this regularly? Discard office supplies you haven't used in over a year. You can always get more. Don't say, "You never know, I might need this someday".
- Does someone else have this information or is it already filed somewhere? Is this spare copy needed?
- Does this piece of equipment work properly? Throw out old pens and markers that don't work.
- Is this the most recent copy? Throw out old business cards, pamphlets, letterhead.
- Open new files for anything of importance you want to keep that does not have an obvious home.
- Just keep one stapler, three hole punch or tape dispenser. Give away all duplicate office tools.

"Your imagination is your preview of life's coming attractions."
Albert Einstein

Reduce Reading Time

"We should be careful to get out of an experience only the wisdom that is in it, stop there, lest we be like the cat that sits on a hot stove lid. She will never sit down on a hot stove lid again; but she will never sit down on a cold one either."
                                                                Mark Twain

Reading and writing reports, memos, letters, books, journals, papers and other business documents take up a significant amount of everyone's work day. Fortunately, there are plenty of simple techniques for improving your skill in these two core areas.

Carefully Choose Reading Material
Ask yourself first: What is my purpose in reading this material? Does it bring me closer to my goals? Don't waste time browsing through newspapers or magazines. Identify articles of relevance and go directly there. Resist the temptation to be distracted by interesting but irrelevant articles.

Mail
- Don't even open envelopes that are clearly junk mail ... recycle them immediately.
- Open mail directly over a wastebasket so you can immediately trash what's not needed.
- Handle each item only once, and decide what action to take, even if it's only where to file.
- Batch your mail and incoming basket all at once for   greater productivity.
- For a speedy response, make a brief comment on the original letter or memo, and fax it back, or make a copy and return it with a post-it note.

"I read part of it all the way through."
Samuel Goldwyn

Improve your reading skills
Research suggests the average reading speed is only 200 words per minute against a possible 1000 words per minute. Many of us needlessly slow down our reading speed by reading every word and silently turning words into sounds inside our head, neither of which are necessary.

Read Faster
- Being conscious of how much time you take to read will automatically have you read faster.
- Rapid readers use their hand or a guide to pace themselves down a page.
- Don't read an entire line - simply identify whatever words you are able to as

your eyes move across and down each page. Look for key information.
- It might feel uncomfortable at first, but you'll be amazed at how much you actually understand and retain, and how much time you'll save.

Reading Books and Reports

Make a point of skimming the introduction, preface, and the table of contents, these will help you quickly identify and investigate only the areas that meet your purposes. Get a general idea of the book's structure and content. Chapter headings, section headings within chapters, charts, illustrations and captions help locate areas of significance. The first and last paragraph of chapters or sections often provide clues about their content. Skim each chapter one at a time, identifying key areas worthy of reading further. After that, go back and explore these key areas further, continuing to evaluate the content against your reading goals. Be ruthless about moving on quickly. When you read something meaningful, something you'll take action on or wish to discuss, write out your point or question in the margin.

Change gears as you read
- Skimming to find short answers to who, what, where, when questions
- Scanning to answer more complex questions, why and how
- Studying in detail for deeper meaning and understanding

"Some books are to be tasted, others to be swallowed, and some few to be chewed and digested."
Francis Bacon

Checklist to Reduce Reading
- Ask yourself which periodicals offer the most information or value for the least reading time? Eliminate the 'nice-to-know' ones.
- Practice the 'rip and file' technique. Skim magazine contents, pull articles that might be valuable, file them under their particular subject for future reading when the issue becomes a priority. Or even better, just highlight them and delegate the 'rip and file' to your assistant.
- Circulate journals among your team members, with a routing slip that has your name at the end. Encourage them to highlight, or make margin notes of interesting items. If it comes back to you with few entries, consider eliminating it. Scan any notations when the publication is returned.
- Schedule reading sessions for late afternoon or early evening - the 'low' part of your day.
- Keep a reading folder tucked away in your briefcase to review during taxi rides, commutes, or time waiting.
- If reading matter continues to pile up, consider tossing any publications that have been around for more than 6 weeks.
- Learn to skim. Read headlines, check section headings on reports, skim

relevant material only for key ideas, highlight critical points or paragraphs and write notes in margins.

- Learn rapid or speed reading.
- Delete your name from the internal routing list of any material that is not critical.
- Delegate your assistant to toss material you don't need to read, or to review and highlight relevant sections of need-to-read articles.

> *"When you stop learning, stop listening, stop looking and asking questions, always new questions, then it is time to die."*
> Lillian Smith

Rapid Writing

"Writing is easy. All you do is sit staring at a blank sheet of paper until the drops of blood form on your forehead."

Gene Fowler

For many people, writing even a brief memo can be a time-consuming nightmare. They procrastinate and stare at their monitor or blank piece of paper. They search desperately for the right words, write a few lines, then delete them. Again, there are practical steps you can take to improve the speed and efficiency with which text is produced.

Decrease your writing time

Most people spend far too much time crafting their response. Consider using the telephone to answer mail. If you do have to write something, be clear about what you want to say. Establish the specific purpose of your text. Save time by using previous letters as templates that you call up every time you need t write a similar one.

Getting started

The toughest part is writing the first few words. Once your mind is engaged, the right words seem to come automatically. Try writing exactly what comes into your mind then edit it later. When you start, don't worry about getting the content 100% correct. Allow your ideas to flow rapidly, even at the expense of sloppy sentences and spelling.

Key it in right away - don't write in longhand then transfer it to a computer. Doing it once, and getting it right the first time saves immeasurable time. For letters and memos, eliminate the first draft.

> *"The enemy came. He was beaten. I am tired. Good night."*
> Vicomte de Turenne after the Battle of Dunen, 1658 A.D.

131

Maintain a rapid pace

Keep your creative juices flowing. Don't stop reread what you have written - that can cause writer's block. Make your text adequate, not perfect. If your communication is clear and to the point, that's good enough. Remember to use logic and structure. Your reader must be able to follow your explanations and ideas as rapidly and easily as possible.

Keep it short

Banish words or phrases which add nothing to your message such as;
- it goes without saying
- It's hardly necessary to repeat
- I'd like to begin by saying
- I feel sure you will understand

Digital Ditties

- Use an alias or shortcut on your desktop to quickly open up documents that you require regularly..
- Diligently utilize spell and grammar check
- Save immediately and save often. Set up your computer to save automatically every 2 minutes.
- Save backup copies of larger documents to a separate disk as you work on them
- Ensure your files and folders are organized so that you can retrieve and store documents quickly.

"If what you did yesterday still looks big to you today, then you haven't done much today."
Unknown

Personal Habits Exercises
Do You Procrastinate?

How successful are you at managing procrastination? Use this self-test to determine if you have a problem with procrastination. Answer Yes or No to each question.

1. I intentionally do the things I find most distasteful early in the day. . . . .   Yes   No

2. When tempted to put off tasks I set a deadline for myself, including a starting time. . . . .   Yes   No

3. I break large assignments into smaller manageable tasks and tackle a few at a time. . . . .   Yes   No

4. I know the kinds of things I regularly put off. . . . .   Yes   No

5. I delegate tasks and/or functions that aren't worthy of my time. . . . .   Yes   No

6. When facing a difficult problem of procrastination, I "go public" by announcing my deadline and asking others to hold me accountable. . . . .   Yes   No

7. I reward myself when accomplishing difficult or distasteful tasks. . . . .   Yes   No

8. I rarely have to be reminded of a deadline. . . . .   Yes   No

9. I feel really uncomfortable putting things off. . . . . .   Yes   No

Add how many times you answered yes.

0-3 You have a serious problem with procrastination. Solving this problem should be an absolute priority for you.
4-6   You could improve your tendency to procrastinate in several ways
7 + You have no trouble with procrastination and don't need any further direction.

Eliminate Your Procrastination Now

The only real cure for procrastination is to develop the Do It Now habit. Individuals that have trouble getting started, or find it difficult to bring themselves to do certain things without a looming deadline need to develop a strong sense of urgency. You need to say to yourself Do It Now, and then actually Do It Now. Honour yourself so that every time you tell yourself to Do It Now you follow through.

1. What have you been postponing that you know you should do?

_____

2. Is it important?

_____

3. Do you need to do it at all?

_____

4. If so, what is stopping you from Doing it Now?

_____

5. If it must be done tell yourself to **Do it Now**, put down your pen or pencil and go **Do it Now**. Or Commit yourself to doing it first thing tomorrow morning ... not after your coffee, not after checking your email ... first thing tomorrow!

Perfectionism Test

The most common waste of time among high achievers is the passion for perfection. Individuals that are driven to be the best rise to positions of power and influence, yet at times render themselves ineffective because what's good enough for a particular situation is not good enough for them.

If you (or others) consider yourself a perfectionist try these three exercises. Don't look at each rating until after you've completed the exercise. Discuss your ratings with those of importance around you and see if they agree that your drive for perfection actually renders you less effective.

1. Draw a picture of a man in front of his house. Do this before reading any further.

Ratings
a) Perfect for the situation: Stick man and a box that takes less than 10 seconds

b) A little more than needed: A chimney, hands, feet, fingers, that takes 10-15 seconds
c) Far more too much time and effort: Any additional detail or taking more than 15 seconds, your life, your livelihood and your priorities don't depend on how good this looks.

2. Write a synopsis of your day from when you got up to when you got to work. Do this before reading any further.

Ratings
a) Perfect for the situation: 6 words (Got up, ate, drove to work)
b) A little more than needed: 9 words (Got up at 6:30, showered, dressed, drove to work)
c) Far too much time and effort: More than 9 words; time spent on details is time you can't spend on your existing priorities

3. Realistic exercise:.

Look at the tasks you complete for one full day. Decide what would be adequate for each situation? What is the minimum requirement for each task or activity. What could you spend less time on, enabling you to spend more time working towards meaningful goals, bringing you closer to achieving what you want in life. Write out the things that you've decided you spend too much time on, and commit to doing only what is required in each situation.

_____

_____

_____

_____

_____

_____

_____

_____

_____

_____

Three Day Powerful Listening Exercise

Powerful listening significantly increases performance and productivity. By exercising the fundamentals of powerful listening you will reduce misunderstandings, save time and generate ideas and actions that bring you closer to achieving the most important things in your life.

Day One
Practice these powerful listening skills in each of your conversations.
- Concentrate completely, drop everything
- Listen for what's important
- Be courteous
- Listen with your whole body

Who did you really listen to today

Day Two
Practice these powerful listening skills in each of your conversations.
- Concentrate completely, drop everything
- Keep an open mind
- Identify and ignore prejudices
- Avoid the temptation to interrupt

Who did you really listen to today

Day Three
Practice these powerful listening skills in each of your conversations.
- Concentrate completely, drop everything
- Don't overreact emotionally
- Take notes to reinforce your understanding
- Clarify what's relevant
- Reinforce the speaker

Who did you really listen to today

Do You Have Trouble Saying No?

How successful are you at saying No? Use this self-test to determine if you have a problem with saying No. Answer Yes or No to each question.

1. When I am asked by someone to do them a favour I don't feel right saying No. . . . .   Yes   No

2. I have too much on my plate right now. . . . .   Yes   No

3. I hardly ever insist on someone seeing me later. . . .   Yes   No

4. When someone asks if I have "a minute" I usually oblige. . . . .   Yes   No

5. When I say yes without thinking and recognize I've made a mistake, I still go ahead with the request. . .   Yes   No

6. When I am overloaded I just try to work harder or longer. . . . .   Yes   No

7. I don't know how to say no politely. . . . .   Yes   No

8. I have never said No to my boss . . . .   Yes   No

9. I'm unsure of what I should be doing most of the time, and can't evaluate additional requests on my time.   Yes   No

10. I don't have much time for myself. . . . .   Yes   No

Add how many times you answered yes.

0-3   You say No quite well and don't need any further direction.
4-6   You could improve your ability to say No in several areas.
7 +   You have a serious problem with saying No. Solving this problem should be an absolute priority for you.

Are You and Your Work Space Organized?

How successful are you at keeping yourself and your work space organized? Use this self-test to determine how organized you are. Answer Yes or No to each question.

1. I keep important tools within easy reach; planner/organizer, computer, working files, telephone, calculator, phone directory, pen. . . . .   Yes   No

2. My desk is clear of all but the task I am working on.   Yes   No

3. I have a system for recording in one place everything that I have to do or remember. . . . .   Yes   No

4. I rarely forget to do things I've committed to doing   Yes   No

5. I remove distractions, such as other work on my desk, before starting any task. . . . .   Yes   No

6. My flow of paperwork is controlled to eliminate all unnecessary periodicals, forms, reports, and correspondence. . . . .   Yes   No

7. I have an up-to-date filing system that allows me to retrieve files within a moments notice. . . . .   Yes   No

8. I have a reading file that I carry and refer to when I have a few spare minutes.   Yes   No

9. I have a prioritized action list that I work from every day. . . . .   Yes   No

10. I understand the difference between efficient and effective, and I'm effective. . . . .   Yes   No

Add how many times you answered yes.

0-3 You are seriously unorganized. Solving this problem should be an absolute priority for you. 4-7 You could improve your personal organization in several ways

8 + You are extremely organized and don't need any further direction.

Speed Reading Exercise

Research has found little relationship between reading rate and understanding. Some people read rapidly and with excellent comprehension, while others read painfully slow and have only a poor understanding of the material.

If you're reasonably bright, and have a general comprehension of the language and terms of what you are reading, there's nothing difficult or special about achieving reading speeds of between 800 and 1,000 words per minute. Realize however that Speedreading is not a substitute for rigorous selection of reading material.

Learn to Speedread using a pacer card

When reading, guide your eyes swiftly down a page while skimming or scanning by using a scanning card. If you don't have a card you can use your hand just as effectively. Here's how:

- Place the card, or your hand, flat on the page above a line of of print. Cover what you've read as you move it down the page, which prevents time wasted in backtracking.

- As you move the card down the page, keep your gaze fixed on the line directly beneath it.

- Adjust your reading speed by making the card move slower or faster down the page, while making certain your eyes keep pace with the guide.

- Do not try to read an entire line at once. Instead identify whatever words you are ably to in each line as the card 'pushes' your eyes down the page.

- Try short 'training sessions' during which you increase the speed with which you move the guide.
  You will become comfortable over time, and may be able to maintain a faster reading speed eventually without the guide.

Things to Do
to Develop Positive Habits

1. Think big and start right away.
2. Have integrity, do it because you said you would do it.
3. Go public, tell the world your new habit and ask for support and coaching.
4. Eliminate procrastination.
5. Become a powerful listener.
6. Learn when and how to say No.
7. Clean up the clutter in your workspace.
8. Keep your desk clear of distractions, keep everything off except what you are working on.
9. Touch paper only once, Trash, File, Delegate or Take Action.
10. Be selective about what you read.
11. Read faster, even if it's uncomfortable.
12. Write less, not more.

"Couldn't you hear me knocking?"

Time Management...

Abuse of Your Time

Eliminate Email Overwhelm

Email is by far the most phenomenal time saving invention ever developed for communicating the written word, yet the sheer volume of messages for some people can uncontrollably 'suck up' their time if not used wisely. Be very, very cautious of automatically giving your incoming email higher priority than previously identified actions on your to-do list. Unless you are in a position that is completely reactive, do not let it dictate how you spend large portions of your day.

Effective Email Checklist

Email can be as much a curse as a blessing, becoming a ball and chain instead of a tool . Below you'll find 16 helpful hints, suggestions, tips and facts for email senders and receivers. According to a recent study by MIT, email messages are expected to increase tenfold over the next decade. That means if you are handling 45 minutes of email today, in ten years you'll have 8 hours worth unless you put effective habits and controls in place.

- Evaluate email messages the same as you do standard mail, act, file, forward or trash immediately.

- When responding, consider the reply function immediately with a one sentence response.
- When asking for a response, request that the recipient immediately use the reply function themselves.
- For those with a huge influx and backlog of email, train others to discriminate what they send you.
- It takes an average of three minutes to handle each email message. That means if you send your message to 10 recipients you've created half an hour worth of work.
- Do not let your email time exceed a total of 10-15% of your day (one hour)
- Do not send messages and copies to ensure anyone remotely interested stays informed.
- There are email filters built in to most mail handling programs that can automatically re-direct messages based on the senders name, subject or other such information. Spam Attack is a good one.
- Quick Keys is an email program that allows you to set up one button that will automatically insert a pre-set message informing the recipient of any conclusion or question, forward the message and remove it from your in-box ... all with one click.
- Unsubscribe from electronic newsletters that provide little value.
- Ask to be removed from mailing lists.
  - Jokes are funny, but not when they clog up your in-box.
  - Have an assistant screen, sort, prioritize and forward your email in order of priority.
  - Consider a second private email address for important contacts.
  - If you don't recognize the name of the sender, or the subject doesn't interest or concern you, zap it.
  - Double task ... handle email while you're dialing outgoing phone calls, or on hold.
  - Be succinct; Restrict updates to a sentence or two.
  - Have your people use the subject field to communicate content and priority of messages at-a-glance.
  - Stop sending email simply FYI ... and ask not to be sent documents simply FYI.

"Blessed are ye when ye direct your best efforts to self-training and self-control"
Buddha

Control Interruptions

"Unless you are in the business of making wine or cheese, time is of the essence."

Bumble Dupurs

Develop a militant attitude

The value that you place on your time will control the way others value it and you. It must be stressed again how important self-determination is. Determine whether or not people 'get it' and respect it. If you have something very important to do that you are committed to doing, you must stay focused and not be distracted ... close yourself off from interruptions. Be firm with those who undervalue your time. You can be firm, create respect, and still remain courteous. Think about it, then do it.

Drop in visitors

These unexpected personal interruptions are one of our biggest time wasters because they're so common, and so hard to resist. It could be a friend, colleague, manager, or senior executive ... but it will undoubtedly take more than a minute (the average drop in takes 10 minutes), and the time needed to recover your concentration and your momentum is quite often longer than the actual time consumed by the visit.

Don't invite interruptions

Evaluate your physical location. Are you on a regular office route, does your desk face the aisle? If your physical choices are limited, at least turn your computer away from the entrance to your work space. Get rid of things that invite people into your workspace, like candy jars, unnecessary guest chairs or popular magazines. Be visibly busy to avoid unnecessary interruptions ... discipline yourself to avoid eye contact with pedestrian traffic. Don't look up every time you hear a noise.

"Superior people never make long visits."
Marianne Moore

The habitual chatterbox

Avoid them like the plague. Absolutely refuse to make eye contact when they're hovering. If they catch you off guard, explain you don't mean to be rude, but unfortunately you can't chat right now, you're working on (_____). If it continues try this; "I notice that you usually have a lot to say, and I really have a hard time keeping up with you; I feel somewhat overwhelmed and can't remember everything you are saying or what I was doing. Are you aware that you are doing this? Eventually they'll get the point that you're not easy prey.

What to say when you're interrupted

When someone does get your attention, be courteous but businesslike; acknowledge them, and stop what you're doing to listen. Find out, as specifically as possible, what's on their mind, then depending on the situation, do one of the following:

- Deal with their issue if it is brief or a real emergency
- Set up another time to meet with them "I don't mean to be rude, but I'm in the middle of something right now. I have got about 15 minutes at 4:00 when we could discuss this more effectively. Would that be OK."
- Suggest they see a more appropriate person
- Encourage them to work out a solution on their own. "I have complete faith in your ability to use your own judgement on this one, now if you don't mind I have to get back to (_____)"

Lock yourself up

If you're working on something that takes intense concentration over a significant period of time, don't be afraid to render yourself unavailable. Stop your calls, close your door, use a boardroom, put up a polite or humorous Do Not Disturb sign.

"Few men of action have been able to make a graceful exit at the appropriate time,"
Malcolm Muggeridge

Control time spent in appointments

If you're meeting with someone about work, it's quite common, expected and appropriate to chat for a while. But be responsible and take charge when it is time to move on to business.

If it's a prospect or client, gauge their interest in chatting. There is value in building rapport, in listening to their likes, dislikes, hobbies, family members etc. Allow the social portion of the meeting only for as long as you consider appropriate and valuable, then shift from a relaxed posture to more business like, open your file and say something like, "That's interesting, (or great.) I'd like to hear more about that sometime, but let's get to the work you're paying me for." Be firm but polite.

Control The Telephone

The telephone, when used correctly, is a potent time saver. There are times when you can communicate more rapidly and efficiently by phone than any other means. It enables you to contact people you might otherwise have to travel to see; mistakes and misunderstandings can be cleared up instantly, decisions and progress can be made within moments. However as much as 40% of wasted time in some offices is attributed to poor telephone techniques that do not control the efficiency of a call.

Many of our problems with the telephone involve issues of human nature. That strong tug that says "answer me" comes from our own emotions and beliefs such as:

- Assumption of legitimacy ... we assume every call is a legitimate demand on our time.
- Fear of offending others by not taking their call
- Desire to keep informed, to know what's going on
- Ego - the fact we're called makes us feel important
- Pleasure of socializing
- An excuse for procrastinating on things we don't like.

Control your telephone efficiency
- Set a time limit per call. Use a three minute egg timer.
- Limit social conversation.
- Provide short answers to questions.
- Make sure the key part of the message is remembered
- Refuse to take calls during certain times.
- Complete high-concentration tasks early in the day, either from home or at the office before 9:00 am
- Don't make calls when you're upset. Memory on facts and figures is poor, judgement is clouded, you can't focus enough to avoid time-wasting errors and misunderstandings
- Visualize before making important calls
- Encourage co-operation by asking; "Will that be all right"
- Take the initiative and make the calls, giving you a psychological advantage
- Before calling, always have a clear idea of what you hope to achieve by making the call. Have notes with a checklist of what you have to discuss.
- Telephoning while standing literally heightens your sense of authority while sharpening your mind. It also helps you complete calls faster.
- Refuse to answer every time it rings.
- If you're working uninterrupted, turn off the ringer
- Batch your calls for greater efficiency.
- Concentrate, and practice good listening skills.
- Be determined to generate something of value from every phone call.
- Have all of the information you require in front of you before making the call.
- Leave effective voice mail messages. Leave specific information that completes an interaction; or specific requests that allows the receiver to take action. Never just leave your name and number.

"The great advantage it possesses over every other form of electrical apparatus consists in the fact that it requires no skill to operate"
Alexander
Graham Bell

147

- Start the call on a business footing ... "I know you're busy; I just have one quick question about ..." or "What can I do for you today."
- End your call efficiently. **Be polite**, use their name when saying goodbye. Repeat facts you want remembered. "I just have a minute before I have to go, is there anything else we need to discuss?" **Be firm** ... avoid being drawn into conversation. **Be gone** ... hang up and start dialing next call.
- Use a generic greeting on your Voice Mail that strongly requests a specific message, so you don't have to change it each day. The exception would be when you won't be checking messages
- Don't get caught up in having to check several Voice Mail systems for messages. Try not having Voice Mail on your cell phone.
- Do not use Call Waiting; This lets any incoming call, regardless of its importance, interrupt and interfere with the call you're on. Better that they get a busy signal and call you back or automatically move to your Voice Mail.
- Don't make calls when people are typically out of the office - before 9:00, during lunch, or after 5:00.

"Those who make the worst use of their time are the first to complain about its brevity."

Jean de La Bruyere

Save time for others on the phone

Remember, you'll get others to respect your time on the phone if you have to respect for theirs:

- Never allow your phone to ring more than three times
- Never answer while eating or drinking.
- Never put your hand over the phone.
- If you say you'll phone back, then do so, even if you don't have the required   information yet.
- If you don't have the answer, call them back anyway and tell them when you expect it.
- Always thank the other person for speaking with you.
- Allow callers to hang up before you do.

Ten Telephone Sins

The telephone should primarily be used as a means of efficient communication. Whether you save or waste time on the phone depends on (1) how sensibly you use it, and (2) how willing you are to rid yourself of bad telephone habits. Here's a list of ten top telephone sins according to Lothar J. Siewart who's time management system is used by over 600,000 people worldwide.

1. You're unclear about your objectives
2. You're insufficiently prepared
3. You call at a bad time
4. You have to search for the number

5. You don't have the necessary documents at hand
6. You haven't made any preliminary notes
7. You don't state your purpose clearly
8. You hold a monologue instead of listening and asking questions
9. You don't take any notes
10. You don't come to a definite agreement.

Reduce Time Wasted in Meetings

There's no worst time waster, or one that we feel in less control of, than spending unnecessary time in meetings. Always think long and hard about whether a meeting is really needed at all.

Dr. David Lewis in '10-Minute Time and Stress Management' claims that in the UK alone, more than four million hours, or 450 years, are spent attending meetings every working day. A great portion of these include self-promotion, office politics, staring out the window, doodling and waiting for them to end.

Make it clear that you believe everyone's time is better spent when solutions are reached without meetings. Whenever possible, make routine decisions informally. Hold brief, informal meetings in the corridor, at the coffee machine or in the parking lot. Hold short meetings standing up ... they won't last as long!

> *"I am a great believer, if you have a meeting, in knowing where you want to come out before you start the meeting. Excuse me if that doesn't sound very democratic."*
> Nelson Rockefeller

Before agreeing to meet
- Ask yourself, or your manager if necessary, whether your presence is critical. If not, politely decline attendance ... If so, request to attend only the portion that is.
- Attempt to fulfill the purpose without a meeting, while you are speaking with the person who called it.
- Send a written statement summarizing your views and/or choices as a substitute for attendance.

If you must go, take these responsibilities seriously
- Be prompt, and encourage meetings to start on time
- Be prepared...make sure you have relevant documents and are fully briefed. Bring reading or other work you can do quietly should the conversation become irrelevant to you.
- Be involved...participate in discussions and help keep them on track if possible.
- Be attentive...much time is wasted because people's minds wander and things have to be repeated.
- Be relevant..ensure your remarks, comments and suggestions genuinely address the central issues facing the meeting, and do not merely demonstrate

your wit or wisdom.
- Be brief - say what you need to stay then stop ... avoid rambling on.
- Be courteous ... do not interrupt a speaker.
- Be focused on issues, not individuals. Much time is wasted in meetings when one person attacks another, which is disruptive and unproductive.
- Be action oriented; follow up where a decision has been made which affects you, always act on it as quickly as possible.

Rickover Style Agenda/Minutes

Admiral Hyman Rickover was famous for running tight meetings. He developed a wonderfully concise format that served as both agenda and minutes. At the beginning of the meeting topics were listed by name with a starting time. By the end of the meeting, the decision on each one had been recorded - Yes, No or Hold - responsibility assigned to a particular person, and a deadline established. Rickover would scrawl a big R at the bottom, cross out the word 'Agenda' and write in 'Minutes', and order copies distributed immediately to those with a need to know.

"A committee is a cul-de-sac down which ideas are lured and then quietly strangled."
Sir Barnett Cocks

Agenda/Minutes Rickover Style				
Time	Item	Decision	Responsibility	Deadline
10:00	A	Yes	BJ	9/15
10:20	B	No	~	~
10:35	C	Hold	~	~
10:45	D	No	~	~
10:55	E	Yes	CB	10/1
11:00	Adjourn			

18 Tips to Reduce Meeting Time

Meetings absorb the greatest part of managers' activity and time. Surveys have shown that most managers, depending on their level, spend 50-80% of their time in meetings, and 90% of them claim that half of their meeting time is wasted. Here's what they have to say;

- There are too many meetings
- The wrong people participate
- They are poorly run
- They last too long
- Nothing gets followed up.

Take action on these practical tips and you'll generate greater effectiveness in your meetings.

1. Commit yourself to reducing wasted time in meetings

The best intentions are useless unless backed up by a sincere and resolute commitment to taking the actions necessary to reduce wasted time in meetings. Assume the leadership to create an environment, against all odds, to be more productive. Share your commitment with your boss and your team members, and empower others to share this commitment.

2. Ask yourself if a meeting is really necessary

'The best meetings are the ones that don't have to take place'. Always keep this sentence in mind when deciding on whether to call a meeting. Can you accomplish the same thing with a memo or phone call to all participants. Are you holding the meeting out of habit rather than need. Could regular meetings be every other week instead of weekly. If someone calls and asks to get together to discuss something, ask, "Could we just make a decision right now on the phone?"

3. Find out if you have to take part personally

Is it possible to decline a meeting invitation without missing anything of importance? Would simply receiving the minutes keep you suitably informed? Can you send a representative?

4. Limit your participation to the extent it is needed then excuse yourself.

If you must attend, scrutinize the agenda to determine what items directly impact you or your department and require your participation. Respectfully inform the chair that unfortunately you will only be present for those agenda items that you've identified.

> *"Meetings are indispensable when you don't want to do anything."*
> John Kenneth Galbraith

5. Prepare an agenda, with time limits for each topic

Once you've done this, go back and cut the time allotted to each issue by 25%, then circulate the agenda in advance. Put the start time for each item so that participants will have the option to come for issues that directly relate to them.

6. Restrict the number of participants to those who are absolutely necessary.

Discourage participants from bringing assistants or observers whose time could be better spent on achieving objectives. Participants should be restricted to those directly affected by any decisions, those with specific knowledge, those who are making the decisions, those with related experience, those respected advisors and problem solvers.

7. Start on time
If you delay a meeting for latecomers, you reward them and penalize those on time. Levy a token 'late fine' of a toonie for latecomers that you can accumulate for charity. If it's not your meeting, say something like "Howard is probably tied up on the phone. Why don't we get started, and when he gets here we can fill him in." Then when Howard arrives, summarize: "We could tell you had been held up, so we've gone ahead and discussed _____, here are the highlights of what you missed." A good manager they will appreciate this.

8. Always announce the cost-per-hour of this meeting
And proclaim your intention that it will be efficient and be convincing in stating that it will be successful. No other activity costs as much in wasted time as meetings. Use this calculation to determine how much each of your meetings costs per hour and communicate the value before each meeting starts.

Cost per Hour Calculation for Meetings
Yearly Income + Benefits (35%) / 1200 effective hours per year = cost per hour
Calculate the approximate accumulated cost per hour of all your meeting participants.

Yearly income	Cost per effective hour
$25,000	$28
$35,000	$39
$50,000	$56
$75,000	$85
$100,000	$113
$125,000	$141
$150,000	$169

9. Establish rules of cooperation
Such things as an agreement limiting each contributor to 30 or 60 seconds, or the process for passing resolutions.

10. Put one participant in charge of keeping time and the minutes. Ensure it is someone with assertiveness skills and empower them to limit discussion to predetermined time limits.

11. Stick to the agenda
Establish time limits for each item and individual comments; once the allotted time is up, move on to the next item. When people realize you are serious about this, the discussions will become much more focused

12. Dismiss participants who are no longer needed
When possible, organize the agenda around people involved in the topics. Release people as soon as their topics have been dealt with. This saves their time, and further limits time needed for discussing subsequent topics.

13. Stay on track
Keep socializing to a minimum, bring discussion back on topic when it strays, look for and curtail repetition, block such 'killer phrases' as "We've never done it that way."

14. Repeat decisions and responsibility for action
This ensures participant's consent, rules out misunderstandings, and saves time on follow-up.

15 . Limit breaks
Break for a maximum of 10 minutes, and not before one hour and 45 minutes of straight meeting time. Any meeting scheduled for two hours or less should have no breaks. Longer meetings should break only once every two hours. If need be, get everyone to stand up and stretch for 30 seconds, but not leave their place at the table. Don't give in to smokers. Let them smoke on their time, not yours.

16. End meetings early if possible
If you finish all agenda items early, end the meeting right then and there. Don't chit-chat or add new items just because you have found time.

17. Don't keep participants longer than you've agreed
Nobody wants to be under the pressure of deadlines caused by meetings that run over. Ensure that the most important items are discussed at the beginning and that relatively unimportant issues remain unfinished. Finish the meeting no later than when it is scheduled to finish.

18. Prepare minutes that clearly summarize the meeting
If possible, distribute minutes within 24 hours outlining action to be taken and individual responsible. Even better, use the Rickover Style of immediate minutes.

Productive Meetings

Meetings that go off track and waste people's time are usually those that have no clear objective, rules of order that are not followed, or concern themselves with issues other than productivity. Here are some suggestions on how to hold meetings that concern themselves with generating productivity.

Productivity Factors
References to productivity refer to the following factors
1. Providing deliverables
2. Generating productivity in others
3. Leadership initiatives
4. Client satisfaction
5. Planning
6. Implementation and action
7. Identifying and removing barriers to productivity
8. Developing systems that improve effectiveness.

Meeting Objectives
1. Discussions will be restricted to activities that impact team productivity.
2. Listen for potential duplication of effort and means of increasing effectiveness.
3. Uncover additional opportunities to support team productivity.
4. Uncover barriers to team productivity.
5. Determine action items, responsibility, and implementation deadlines.

"You may ask me for anything you like except time."
Napoleon Bonaparte

Rules of Order
1. Be prompt, as meetings will start exactly as scheduled.
2. Review the agenda and limit your attendance to items that effect you not interest you.
3. Come prepared with appropriate documents and questions.
4. Be relevant with your comments; avoid going off-track or debating issues.
5. Be concise; say what you need to say then stop.
6. Be courteous; avoid interrupting others.
7. Be action oriented; look for, and record actions that improve productivity.
8. Restrict discussions to the time allotted for each agenda item.
9. Honour the timekeeper; acknowledge a three minute warning signal for the end of discussion on each topic.

Fru-Fru or Everything Left Over

"Everything comes to him who hustles while he waits."

Thomas Edison

The Outward Bound Wilderness School taught me the phrase fru-fru' which refers to all that loose stuff that isn't put away when you're emptying your canoe for a portage. This is all the stuff that was too good to pass up but didn't easily fit into any modules.

Punctuality

Punctuality provides personal power. Be where you're supposed to be, when you're supposed to be there, as promised, without exception, without excuse, every time, all the time. You cannot expect or hope to have others treat your time with respect if you show little or no respect for theirs. If you are not punctual, you have no leverage or moral authority.

Lie down with dogs, wake up with fleas

Who you hang out with does matter. No matter how strong you think your character is, you can't help but be influenced by the people with whom you hang around; hang around with those of nominal integrity and you'll soon find yourself lying, cheating, conniving and abusing with greater ease and less guilt. Hang around with people who place little value on time (theirs and others) and your own productivity will diminish.

"Training is everything. The peach was once a bitter almond; cauliflower is nothing but cabbage with a college education."

Samuel L. Clemens

Avoid alibi-itis

Underachievers fail to advance because they're too busy whining about how unfair everything is, making excuses for their underachievement. We are not entitled to anything except opportunity and possibility, not even a level playing field. Nothing. Just opportunity and possibility. Eric Hoffer wrote "There are many who find a good alibi far more attractive than an achievement". Don't make excuses ... just do it.

When you fail to reach your goal

If we miss a goal it is not called failure - we only fail ourselves when we don't try. One high achiever defies logic by setting a similar but bigger, more exciting goal with a new appropriate time line.

155

Dealing with busy people

Busy people do not have the least interest in your product, your company, your credibility or your projects. Speak to their self interest ... be other-oriented not product and process oriented. Match your message to their fears, concerns, desires, to the gap that exists between where they are and where they want to be.

What's your time worth?

To truly appreciate what your time is worth, calculate it using this formula. Approximately 30% of our time is actually used in productive actions. This means that based on a 40 hour work week and 3 weeks of holidays, we spend 588 hours a year on productive activities. If you want to make $100,000 per year, your time is worth $170 per hour. Is what you are doing right now worth $170 per hour?

Flexibility

Keep an open mind about the ways a job might get done. Avoid rigid thinking. Don't take refuge in excuses for avoiding new work habits such as "we've always done it this way" Remember what passes as common sense is often stupidity hardened into habit.

Avoid wasting time waiting

- Always confirm your appointment.
- Organize to minimize travel time.
- Never enter the reception area more than five minutes before your appointment. Best to arrive in the parking lot early and work in your car.
- Allow for a margin of error. (I'll see you around 3:30)
- Make sure your arrival is announced.
- Avoid having to repeat your name by having a card ready to hand to the receptionist.
- Keep yourself busy - pull out your reading file or organize your thoughts on paper.

Time Abuse Exercises

How Well Do You Use The Telephone

How effective are you on the telephone? Use this self-test to determine if you have a problem with using the phone. Answer Yes or No to each question.

1. My phone calls are screened effectively.	Yes	No
2. I limit my telephone calls with a three minute egg timer, or a reminder from my assistant	Yes	No
3. Before accepting a phone call, I ask its purpose in order to determine its relative priority	Yes	No
4. I resist the urge to answer every time the phone rings.	Yes	No
5. When working on something that requires my undivided attention, I unplug or forward my calls.	Yes	No
6. Before making a phone call I make sure I have all of the pertinent information required right in front of me.	Yes	No
7. I leave specific action oriented voice mail messages,	Yes	No
8. My own voice mail recording asks for a specific message and is only changed when I'm away from the office and not checking it.	Yes	No
9. I refrain from making outgoing calls when people are not usually in the office.	Yes	No
10. I group most of my outgoing calls and make them one after another.	Yes	No

Add how many times you answered yes

0-3 You have a serious problem with the telephone. Solving this problem should be an absolute priority for you.
4-7 You could improve your use of the telephone in several ways
8 + You are extremely adept on the phone and don't need any further direction.

Do You Waste Time in Meetings?

How successful are you at managing your meeting time? Use this self-test to determine if you have a problem with wasting time in meetings. Answer Yes or No to each question.

1. I resist attending others' meetings in which the purpose is unclear.............................	Yes	No
2. Our meetings have agendas that are time limited for each topic.....................................	Yes	No
3. Our meetings start on time, even if not everyone is present.	Yes	No
4. I often attend only the portions of meetings that are appropriate for me.	Yes	No
5. My boss and my staff are clear that I am committed to resolving issues without wasting time in meetings. ...	Yes	No
6. When someone suggests we should have a meeting, I am clear that it is absolutely required before agreeing..	Yes	No
7. Our meetings always end on time, and quite often end early...	Yes	No
8. Our meetings have very few breaks, and when we do it is for no more than 10 minutes.	Yes	No
9. We refuse to hold regular weekly meetings if there is little of value to discuss.	Yes	No
10. We have an active timekeeper at our meetings.. ...	Yes	No

Add how many times you answered yes

0-3 You waste considerable time in meetings. Solving this problem should be an absolute priority for you.

4-7 You could reduce time wasted in meetings in several ways

8 + You run extremely effective meetings and don't need any further direction.

Things To Do
to Stop Abuse of Your Time

1. Don't let incoming email dictate your priorities or overwhelm you.
2. Close your door when you are working, and close it often.
3. Don't give up your time every time someone asks if you have a few minutes.
4. Refuse to answer the phone when you are with someone, or working on anything that requires concentration.
5. Make as many decisions as possible without meetings
6. If you must attend a meeting, attend only the portion that applies to you.
7. Focus your action and attention on activities that provide the greatest return, and feel good about it.
8. Don't put up with unnecessary red tape or delays.
9. Confidently close yourself off when you require concentration on anything. Find a boardroom, work from home or post a 'Do Not Disturb' sign

"They've cut the water off, and I
need some to cook the potatoes..."

chapter nine

Completion Excercises

Post-Workbook Avoidance Strategies

If you've been honest with yourself throughout this book and exercises you realize that ultimately you are responsible for your entire life. Only you can make a difference. We'd like you to do a different version of the exercise that you completed at the beginning of the book, identifying some of the ways in which you could avoid being successful in managing yourself through time.

This time, list some of the techniques that you could easily neglect implementing once the daily challenges of your job begin to overwhelm you. The things you know would help you become more effective, but you probably won't have the discipline to practice regular enough to become habits. List the first ten that come to mind, then go back and number them in order of their likelihood of occurring.

Avoidance Strategy   **Order of Probability**

_____   # _____

_____   # _____

_____ # _____
_____ # _____
_____ # _____
_____ # _____
_____ # _____
_____ # _____
_____ # _____

Here are some sample answers given by seminar participants

- Won't plan every day before coming in to the office
- Will write my action list, but not bother to prioritize it.
- Spend more time on something than the situation requires
- Ignore entries in my dayplanner
- Answer every phone call
- Not communicate my commitment to utilizing my time more effectively
- Accept new tasks without thinking (can't say no)
- Neglect my goals and critical success factors when deciding to do something.
- Have little self-discipline
- Incomplete or inadequate delegation
- Be distracted by other thoughts while working on a task (not present to the moment)
- Not taking time to recharge myself
- Letting my work space get out of control
- Not having a sense of urgency

Four Week Behavioural Contract

This contract has you agree to practice your most difficult new habits for 21 days, and reward yourself for doing it.

Take your avoidance strategies from the previous exercise and promise yourself rewards for doing them. Your rewards can come from the previous reward checklist you completed, or they can be completely new ones. The power is in completing this contract with yourself, and then following through on the rewards once you accomplish what you set out to.

Effective Dates: From _____ To _____ .

Signature _____

Achievements Rewards

When I _____ Then I _____

When I _____ Then I _____

When I _____ Then I _____

When I _____ Then I _____

When I _____ Then I _____

When I _____ Then I _____

When I _____ Then I _____

When I _____ Then I _____

When I _____ Then I _____

When I _____ Then I _____

"Look, you're 103 years old,
you've got to start taking better
care of yourself."

chapter ten

What Do I Do Now?

You've done the work and realized the benefits. Some things may seem to have barely improved, and some things got significantly better. You are feeling less stress, you are more productive, and you are seeing the joy in more moments. Maybe you've even begun to create a life that you love.

Celebrate your successes ... relish your achievements. Don't be in such a rush to do more that you miss the opportunity to recognize and reward what you have already accomplished.

Don't backslide ... practice the techniques that work for you to the point they become habits. Use the skills that you have developed to serve you for the rest of your life. Set new goals once you've reached the old ones, use your found time to learn or do something you've always dreamed of, develop your connection with the universe and all that it has to offer.

Do what you can, where you can, and accept your shortcomings as easily as your achievements. Live with faith and purpose, learn from your mistakes and do a little better each day. Take time each day to smell the roses in your life ... the beauty of this world is yours to discover, and you discover more of it when your eyes are truly open.

Resources

Boone, Louis E - *'Quotable Business'*, Random House, New York, 1998

Canfield, Hansen, Hewitt - *'The Power of Focus'*, Health Communications, Deerfield Beach, 2000

Covey, Stephen R. - *'First Things First'*, Covey Leadership Center, Utah, 1998

Dyer, Wayne W. - *'Your Erroneous Zones'*, Funk & Wagnells, New York, 1976

Ellwood, Mark - *'A Complete Waste of Time'*, Pace Productivity, Toronto, 1997

Godwin, Malcolm - *'Who Are You'*, Penguin Books, London, 2000

Goleman, Daniel - *'Working with Emotional Intelligence'*, Bantam, New York, 1998

Gray, John - *'How to Get What You Want and Want What You Have'*, HarperCollins Publishers, New York, 1999

Heider, John - *'The Tao of Leadership'*, Bantam Books, 1986

Hill, Napoleon, and Stone, W. Clement - *'Success Through a Positive Mental Attitude'*, Simon & Schuster, N.Y., 1977

Kennedy, Dan - *'No B.S. Time Management'*, Self Counsel Press, Washington, 1996

Lakein, Alan - *'How to Get Control of Your Time and Your Life'*, Signet Books, New York, 1974

LeBoeuf, Michael - *'Working Smarter'*, Nightingale Conant, Chicago, 1986

Lewis, Dr. David - *'10 Minute Time and Stress Management'*, Piatkus Publishers, London, 1995

Mackenzie, Alec - *'The Time Trap'*, American Management Association, New York, 1990

Neidhardt, Dr. Joseph - *'Managing Stress'*, Self-Counsel Press, Vancouver, 1985

Outward Bound Wilderness School - *'Winds from the Wilderness'*, Toronto, 1989

Peale, Norman Vincent - *'Treasury of Courage and Confidence'*, Doubleday, New York, 197

Pedler, Mike, and Boydell, Tom - *'Managing Yourself'*, Fontana, London, 1989

Seiwert, Lothar J. - *'Time Is Money:Save It'*, Richard D. Irwin Inc, West Germany, 1989

Sharma, Robin - *'The Monk Who Sold His Ferrari'*, HarperCollins, Toronto, 1997

Sharma, Robin - *'Who Will Cry When You Die'*, HarperCollins, Toronto, 1999

Templeton, Charles - *'Succeeding'*, Nightingale Conant,

Tracy, Brian - *'The Psychology of Achievement'*, Nightingale Conant, Chicago, 1988

About The Author

Eugene Dupuis is founder and principal of The Achievement Institute, and a respected subject matter expert. He's a scholar, author, trainer, and mentor who uses a practical mix of success skills and inspirational guidance to develop executives across Canada.

His interest in personal development began at the age of 13 while reading Norman Vincent Peale, Napoleon Hill, and Dale Carnegie. He's studied and applied the teachings of Wayne Dyer, Zig Zigler, Brian Tracy, Deepak Chopra, Tom Peters, Stephen Covey, and many others to transform individuals and organizations.

The former Director of Sales and Marketing for TORSTAR Newspaper Group's six Toronto suburban newspapers, Eugene has worked with executives in some of the country's most prestigious private and public organizations, including TORSTAR, Southam Newspaper Group, Sun Media Corporation, Toronto Life Magazine, The Canadian International Development Agency, the Department of Indian Affairs and Northern Development, and Human Resources Development Canada.

'Time and Self Management; The Master's Program' was recognized by Canada's largest training organization (OSTD) as one of the best training programs in Ontario in 2001. As well as writing and coaching, Eugene conducts powerful group workshops and inspiring keynote presentations. He can be reached at Eugene@Achievement-Institute.ca